Ultimate One Minute Manager

The Ultimate One Minute Manager

Kenneth Blanchard, Ph.D.
Spencer Johnson, M.D.
Robert Lorber
William Oncken Dr.
Hal Burrows
Donald Carew
Eunice Parisi-Carew

Grafton

This omnibus edition published in 2002
by HarperCollins*Publishers*

HarperCollins*Publishers*
77-85 Fulham Palace Road,
Hammersmith, London W6 8JB
www.fireandwater.com

The One Minute Manager
Copyright © Blanchard Family Partnership and
Candle Communications Corporation, 1981, 1982, 1983

Putting the One Minute Manager to Work
Copyright © Blanchard Management Corporation
and RL Lorber Family Trust 1983

The One Minute Manager Meets the Monkey
Copyright © Blanchard Family Partnership and the
William Oncken Corporation 1989

The One Minute Manager Builds High Performing Teams
Copyright © Blanchard Family Partnership.
Don Carew and Eunice Parisi-Carew 1990

The Author asserts the moral right to
be identified as the author of this work

ISBN 0 00 765807 9

Printed and bound in Great Britain by
Omnia Books Limited, Glasgow

All rights reserved. No part of this publication may be
reproduced, stored in a retrieval system, or transmitted,
in any form or by any means, electronic, mechanical,
photocopying, recording or otherwise, without the prior
permission of the publishers.

This book is sold subject to the condition that it shall not,
by way of trade or otherwise, be lent, re-sold, hired out or
otherwise circulated without the publisher's prior consent
in any form of binding or cover other than that in which it
is published and without a similar condition including this
condition being imposed on the subsequent purchaser.

The One Minute Manager

Kenneth Blanchard, Ph.D.
Spencer Johnson, M.D.

The Symbol

The One Minute Manager's symbol – a one minute readout from the face of a modern digital watch – is intended to remind each of us to take a minute out of our day to look into the faces of the people we manage. And to realize that *they* are our most important resources.

Contents

The Search *11*
The One Minute Manager *17*
The First Secret: One Minute Goals *25*
One Minute Goals: Summary *34*
The Second Secret: One Minute Praisings *36*
One Minute Praisings: Summary *44*
The Appraisal *47*
The Third Secret: One Minute Reprimands *50*
One Minute Reprimands: Summary *59*
The One Minute Manager Explains *61*
Why One Minute Goals Work *65*
Why One Minute Praisings Work *76*
Why One Minute Reprimands Work *86*
The New One Minute Manager *99*
A Gift to Yourself *101*
A Gift for Others *105*

Acknowledgments *108*
About the Authors *110*

Introduction

In this brief story, we present you with a great deal of what we have learned from our studies in medicine and in the behavioural sciences about how people work best with other people.

By 'best', we mean how people produce valuable results, and feel good about themselves, the organization and the other people with whom they work.

This allegory, *The One Minute Manager*, is a simple compilation of what many wise people have taught us and what we have learned ourselves. We recognize the importance of these sources of wisdom. We also realize that the people who work with you as their manager will look to you as one of *their* sources of wisdom.

We trust, therefore, that you will take the practical knowledge you gain from this book and use it in your daily management. For as the ancient sage, Confucius, advises each of us: 'The essence of knowledge is, having it, to use it'.

We hope you enjoy *using* what you learn from *The One Minute Manager* and that, as a result, you and the people you work with will enjoy healthier, happier and more productive lives.

Kenneth Blanchard, Ph.D.
Spencer Johnson, M.D.

The One Minute Manager

ONCE there was a bright young man who was looking for an effective manager.

He wanted to work for one. He wanted to become one.

His search had taken him over many years to the far corners of the world.

He had been in small towns and in the capitals of powerful nations.

He had spoken with many managers: with government administrators and military officers, construction superintendents and corporate executives, university professors and shop stewards, with the managers of shops and stores, of restaurants, banks and hotels, with men and women – young and old.

He had gone into every kind of office, large and small, luxurious and sparse, with windows and without.

He was beginning to see the full spectrum of how people manage people.

But he wasn't always pleased with what he saw.

He had seen many 'tough' managers whose organizations seemed to win while their people lost.

Some of their superiors thought they were good managers.

Many of their subordinates thought otherwise.

As the man sat in each of these 'tough people's' offices, he asked, 'What kind of a manager would you say you are?'

Their answers varied only slightly.

'I'm an autocratic manager – I keep on top of the situation', he was told. 'A bottom-line manager.' 'Hard-nosed.' 'Realistic.' 'Profit-minded.'

He heard the pride in their voices and their interest in results.

The man also met many 'nice' managers whose people seemed to win while their organizations lost.

Some of the people who reported to them thought they were good managers.

Those to whom they reported had their doubts.

As the man sat and listened to these 'nice' people answer the same question, he heard:

'I'm a democratic manager'. 'Participative.' 'Supportive.' 'Considerate.' 'Humanistic.'

He heard the pride in their voices and their interest in people.

But he was disturbed.

It was as though most managers in the world were primarily interested either in results or in people.

The managers who were interested in results often seemed to be labelled 'autocratic', while the managers interested in people were often labelled 'democratic'.

The young man thought each of these managers – the 'tough' autocrat and the 'nice' democrat – were only partially effective. 'It's like being half a manager', he thought.

He returned home tired and discouraged.

He might have given up his search long ago, but he had one great advantage. He knew exactly what he was looking for.

'Effective managers', he thought, 'manage themselves and the people they work with so that both the organization and the people profit from their presence'.

The young man had looked everywhere for an effective manager but had found only a few. The few he did find would not share their secrets with him. He began to think maybe he would never find out what really made an effective manager tick.

Then he began hearing marvellous stories about a special manager who lived, ironically, in a nearby town. He heard that people liked to work for this man and that they produced great results together. The young man wondered if the stories were really true and, if so, whether this manager would be willing to share his secrets with him.

Curious, he telephoned the special manager's secretary for an appointment. The secretary put him through immediately.

The young man asked this special manager when he could see him. He heard, 'Any time this week is fine, except Wednesday morning. You pick the time.'

The young man quietly chuckled because this supposedly marvellous manager sounded very strange to him. What kind of manager had that kind of time available? But the young man was fascinated. He went to see him.

WHEN the young man arrived at the manager's office, he found him standing and looking out of the window. When the young man coughed, the manager turned and smiled. He invited the young man to sit down and asked, 'What can I do for you?'

The young man said, 'I'd like to ask you some questions about how you manage people'.

The manager willingly said, 'Fire away'.

'Well, to begin with, do you hold regularly scheduled meetings with your subordinates?'

'Yes, I do – once a week on Wednesdays from 9:00 until 11:00. That's why I couldn't see you then', responded the manager.

'What do you do at those meetings?' probed the young man.

'I listen while my people review and analyse what they accomplished last week, the problems they had, and what still needs to be accomplished. Then we develop plans and strategies for the next week.'

'Are the decisions made at those meetings binding on both you and your staff?' questioned the young man.

'Of course they are', insisted the manager. 'What would be the point of having the meeting if they weren't?'

'Then you are a participative manager, aren't you?' asked the young man.

'On the contrary', insisted the manager, 'I don't believe in participating in any of my staff's decision-making'.

'Then what is the purpose of your meetings?'

'I already told you that', he said. 'Please, young man, do not ask me to repeat myself. It is a waste of my time and yours.

'We're here to get results', the manager continued. 'The purpose of this organization is efficiency. By being organized we are a great deal more productive.'

'Oh, so you're aware of the need for productivity. Then you're more results-oriented than people-oriented', the young man suggested.

'No!' the manager retorted, startling his visitor. 'I hear that all too often.' He got to his feet and began to walk about. 'How on earth can I get results if it's not through people? I care about people *and* results. They go hand in hand.

'Here, young man, look at this.' The manager handed his visitor a plaque. 'I keep it on my desk to remind me of a practical truth.'

*

*People Who Feel
Good About
Themselves*

*Produce
Good Results*

*

Don't make decisions for other people; help them think things through & let them decide.

As the young man looked at the plaque, the manager said, 'Think about yourself. When do you work best? Is it when you feel good about yourself? Or when you don't?'

The young man nodded as he began to see the obvious. 'I get more done when I'm feeling good about myself', he responded.

'Of course you do', the manager agreed. 'And so does everyone else.'

The young man raised his index finger with new-found insight. 'So', he said, 'helping people to feel good about themselves is a key to getting more done'.

'Yes', the manager agreed. 'However, remember productivity is more than just the *quantity* of work done. It is also the *quality*.' He walked over to the window and said, 'Come over here, young man'.

He pointed to the traffic below and asked, 'Do you see how many foreign cars there are on the road?'

The young man looked out of the window and said, 'I see more of them every day. And I suppose that's because they're more economical and they last longer.'

The manager nodded reluctantly and said 'Exactly. So why do you think people are buying foreign cars? Because our manufacturers did not make *enough* cars? Or', the manager said without interrupting, 'because they did not make the *quality* car the public really wanted?'

'Now that I think of it', the young man answered, 'it's a question of *quality* and *quantity*'.

'Of course', the manager added. 'Quality is simply giving people the product or service they really want and need.'

The older man stood at the window lost in his thoughts. He could remember, not so long ago, when Britain and America provided the technology that helped to rebuild Europe and Asia. It still amazed him that they had fallen so far behind in productivity.

The young man broke the manager's concentration. 'I'm reminded of an ad I saw on television', the visitor volunteered. 'It showed the name of the foreign car, and over it came the words *If you're going to take out a long-term car loan, don't buy a short-term car.*'

The manager turned and said quietly, 'I'm afraid that's a rather good summary. And that's the whole point. Productivity is both quantity and quality.'

The manager and his visitor began to walk back towards their chairs. 'And frankly, the best way to achieve both of these results is through people.'

The young man's interest increased. As he sat down, he asked, 'Well, you've already said that you're not a participative manager. Just how would you describe *yourself*?'

'That's easy', he responded without hesitation. 'I'm a One Minute Manager.'

The young man's face showed surprise. He'd never heard of a One Minute Manager. 'You're a what?'

The manager laughed and said, 'I'm a One Minute Manager. I call myself that because it takes very little time for me to get very big results from people.'

Although the young man had spoken with many managers, he had never heard one talk like this. It was hard to believe. A One Minute Manager – someone who gets good results without taking much time.

Seeing the doubt on his face the manager said, 'You don't believe me, do you? You don't believe that I'm a One Minute Manager.'

'I must admit it's hard for me even to imagine', the young man responded.

The manager laughed and said, 'Listen, you'd better talk to my staff if you really want to know what kind of manager I am'.

The manager leaned over and spoke into the office intercom. His secretary, Ms. Metcalfe, came in moments later and handed the young man a sheet of paper.

'Those are the names, positions and phone numbers of the six people who report to me', the One Minute Manager explained.

'Which ones should I talk to?' the young man asked.

'That's your decision', the manager replied. 'Pick any name. Talk to any one of them or all of them.'

'Well, I mean who should I start with?'

'I already told you, I don't make decisions for other people', the manager said firmly. 'Make that decision yourself.' He stood up and walked his visitor towards the door.

'You have asked me, not once, but twice, to make a simple decision for you. Frankly, young man, I find that annoying. Do not ask me to repeat myself. Either pick a name and get started, or take your search for effective management elsewhere.'

The visitor was stunned. He felt uncomfortable, very uncomfortable. A moment of embarrassed silence seemed like an eternity.

Then the One Minute Manager looked the young man in the eye and said, 'You want to know about managing people, and I admire that'. He shook his visitor's hand.

'If you have any questions after talking to some of my people', he said warmly, 'come back and see me. I appreciate your interest and desire to learn how to manage. I would, in fact, like to give you the concept of the One Minute Manager as a gift. Someone gave it to me once and it's made all the difference to me. I want you to understand it fully. If you like it, you may want to become a One Minute Manager yourself someday.'

'Thank you', the young man managed.

He left the manager's office somewhat dumbfounded. As he passed the secretary she said understandingly, 'I can see from your dazed look that you've already experienced our One Minute Manager'.

The young man said very slowly, still trying to work things out, 'I rather think I have'.

'Maybe I can help you', Ms. Metcalfe said. 'I've phoned the six people who report to him. Five of them are here and they have each agreed to see you. You may be better able to understand our One Minute Manager after you've spoken with them.'

The young man thanked her, looked over the list and decided to talk to three of them: Mr. Trenell, Mr. Levy and Ms. Brown.

WHEN the young man arrived at Trenell's office, he found a middle-aged man smiling at him. 'Well, you've been to see the "old man". He's quite a character, isn't he?'

'He seems that way', the young man responded.

'Did he tell you about being a One Minute Manager?'

'He certainly did. It's not true, is it?' asked the young man.

'You'd better believe it is. I hardly ever see him.'

'You mean you never get any help from him?' asked the puzzled young man.

'Essentially very little, although he does spend some time with me at the beginning of a new task or responsibility. That's when he does One Minute Goal Setting.'

'One Minute Goal Setting. What's that?' said the young man. 'He told me he was a One Minute Manager, but he didn't say anything about One Minute Goal Setting.'

'That's the first of the three secrets to One Minute Management', Trenell answered.

'Three secrets?' the young man asked, wanting to know more.

The First Secret: One Minute Goals / 27

'Yes', said Trenell. 'One Minute Goal Setting is the first one and the foundation for One Minute Management. You see, in most organizations when you ask people what they do and then ask their boss, all too often you get two different lists. In fact, in some organizations I've worked in, any relationship between what I thought my job responsibilities were and what my boss thought they were was purely coincidental. And then I would get in trouble for not doing something I didn't even think was my job.'

'Does that ever happen here?' asked the young man.

'No!' Trenell said. 'It never happens here. The One Minute Manager always makes it clear what our responsibilities are and what we are being held accountable for.'

'Just how does he do that?' the young man wanted to know.

'Efficiently', Trenell said with a smile.

Trenell began to explain. 'Once he has told me what needs to be done or we have agreed on what needs to be done, then each goal is recorded on no more than a single page. The One Minute Manager feels that a goal, and its performance standard, should take no more than 250 words to express. He insists that anyone be able to read it within a minute. He keeps a copy and I keep a copy so everything is clear and so we can both periodically check the progress.'

'Do you have these one-page statements for every goal?'

'Yes', answered Trenell.

'Well, wouldn't there be a lot of these one-page statements for each person?'

'No, there really aren't', Trenell insisted. 'The old man believes in the 80-20 goal-setting rule. That is, 80 per cent of your really important results will come from 20 per cent of your goals. So we only do One Minute Goal Setting on that 20 per cent; that is, our key areas of responsibility – maybe three to six goals in all. Of course, in the event a special project comes up, we set special One Minute Goals.'

The First Secret: One Minute

'Interesting', the young man commented. 'I think I understand the importance of One Minute Goal Setting. It sounds like a philosophy of "no surprises" – everyone knows what is expected from the beginning.'

'Exactly', Trenell agreed.

'So is One Minute Goal Setting just understanding what your responsibilities are?' the young man asked.

'No. Once we know what our job is, the manager always makes sure we know what good performance is. In other words, performance standards are clear. He shows us what he expects.'

'How does he show you what he expects?' asked the young man.

'Let me give you an example', Trenell suggested.

The First Secret: One Minute Goals

'One of my One Minute Goals was this: identify performance problems and come up with solutions which, when implemented, will turn the situation around.

'When I first came to work here I spotted a problem that needed to be solved, but I didn't know what to do. So I called the One Minute Manager. When he answered the phone, I said, *I find I have a problem*. Before I could get another word out, he said, *Good! That's what you've been hired to solve*. Then there was a dead silence on the other end of the phone.

'I didn't know what to do. The silence was deafening. I eventually stuttered out, *But I don't know how to solve this problem*.

'*Trenell*, he said, *one of your goals for the future is for you to identify and solve your own problems. But since you are new, come up here and we'll talk*.

'When I got up there, he said, *Tell me, Trenell, what your problem is – but put it in behavioural terms*.

'*Behavioural terms?* I echoed. *What do you mean by behavioural terms?*

'I mean, the manager explained to me, *that I do not want to hear about only attitudes or feelings. Tell me what is happening in observable, measurable terms.*

'I described the problem as best I could.

'He said, *That's good, Trenell! Now tell me what you would like to be happening in behavioural terms.*

'I don't know, I said.

'Then don't waste my time, he snapped.

'I just froze in amazement for a few seconds. I didn't know what to do. He mercifully broke the dead silence.

'If you can't tell me what you'd like to be happening, he said, *you don't have a problem yet. You're just complaining. A problem exists only if there is a difference between what is* actually *happening and what you* desire *to be happening.*

'Being a quick learner, I suddenly realized I knew what I wanted to be happening. After I told him, he asked me to talk about what may have caused the discrepancy between the actual and the desired.

'After that the One Minute Manager said, *Well, what are you going to do about it?*'

'*Well, I could do A*, I said.

'*If you did A, would what you want to happen actually happen?* he asked.

'*No*, I said.

'*Then you have a very bad solution. What else could you do?* he asked.

'*I could do B*, I said.

'*But if you do B, will what you want to happen really happen?* he countered again.

'*No*, I realized.

'*Then, that's also a bad solution*, he said. *What else can you do?*

'I thought about it for a couple of minutes and said, *I could do C. But if I do C, what I want to happen won't happen, so that is a bad solution, isn't it?*

'*Right. You're starting to come around*, the manager then said, with a smile on his face. *Is there anything else you could do?* he asked.

The First Secret: One Minute Goals / 33

'Maybe I could combine some of these solutions,' I said.

'That sounds worth trying,' he said.

'In fact, if I do A this week, B next week and C in two weeks, I'll have it solved. That's fantastic. Thanks so much. You solved my problem for me.'

'He got very annoyed. *I did not,* he interrupted, *you solved it yourself. I just asked you questions – questions you are able to ask yourself. Now get out of here and start solving your own problems on your time, not mine.*

'I knew what he had done, of course. He'd shown me how to solve problems so that I could do it on my own in the future.

'Then he stood, looked me straight in the eye and said, *You're good, Trenell. Remember that the next time you have a problem.*

'I remember smiling as I left his office.'

Trenell leaned back in his chair and looked as if he were reliving his first encounter with the One Minute Manager.

'So', the young man began, reflecting on what he had just heard . . .

One Minute Goal Setting is simply:
1. Agree on your goals.
2. See what good behaviour looks like.
3. Write out each of your goals on a single sheet of paper using less than 250 words.
4. Read and re-read each goal, which requires only a minute or so each time you do it.
5. Take a minute every once in a while out of your day to look at your performance, and
6. See whether or not your behaviour matches your goal.

'That's it', Trenell exclaimed, 'you're a fast learner'.

'Thank you', the young man said, feeling good about himself. 'But let me just jot that down', he said, 'I want to remember that'.

After the young man wrote briefly in the small blue notebook he carried with him, he leaned forward and asked, 'If One Minute Goal Setting is the first secret to becoming a One Minute Manager, what are the other two?'

Trenell smiled, looked at his watch and said, 'Why don't you ask Levy that? You're scheduled to see him this morning too, aren't you?'

The young man was amazed. How did Trenell know that? 'Yes', the young man said as he rose to shake Trenell's hand. 'Thanks so much for your time.'

'You're welcome', Trenell replied. 'Time is one thing I have a lot more of now. As you can probably tell, I'm becoming a One Minute Manager myself.'

As the young man left Trenell's office, he was struck by the simplicity of what he had heard. He thought, 'It certainly makes sense. After all, how can you be an effective manager unless you and your people are sure of what they are being asked to do? And what an efficient way to do it.'

The young man walked the length of the building and took the lift to the second floor. When he got to Mr. Levy's office, he was surprised to meet so young a man. Levy was probably in his late 20s or early 30s. 'Well, you've been to see the "old man". He's quite a character, isn't he?'

He was already getting used to the One Minute Manager being called 'quite a character'.

'I reckon he is', responded the young man.

'Did he tell you about being a One Minute Manager?' asked Levy.

'He certainly did. It's not true, is it?' asked the young man, wondering if he'd get a different answer from Trenell's.

'You'd better believe it's true. I hardly ever see him.'

'You mean you never get any help from him?' asked the young man.

'Essentially very little, although he does spend a fair amount of time with me at the beginning of a new task or responsibility.'

'Yes, I know about One Minute Goal Setting', interrupted the young man.

The Second Secret: One Minute Praisings / 37

'Actually I wasn't thinking so much about One Minute Goal Setting. I was referring to One Minute Praisings.'

'One Minute Praisings?' echoed the young man. 'Are they the second secret to becoming a One Minute Manager?'

'Yes, they are', Levy revealed. 'In fact, when I first started to work here, the One Minute Manager made it very clear to me what he was going to do.'

'What was that?' the visitor asked.

'He said that he knew that it would be a lot easier for me to do well, if I got crystal-clear feedback from him on how I was doing.

'He said he wanted me to succeed. He wanted me to be a big help to the organization, and to enjoy my work.

'He told me that he would try, therefore, to let me know *in no uncertain terms* when I was doing well, and when I was doing poorly.

'And then he cautioned me that it might not be very comfortable at first for either of us.'

'Why?' the visitor asked.

'Because, as he pointed out to me then, most managers don't manage that way and people aren't used to it. Then he assured me that such feedback would be a big help to me.'

'Can you give me an example of what you are talking about?' the young man requested.

'Of course', Levy said. 'Shortly after I started to work, I noticed that, after my manager had done One Minute Goal Setting with me, he would stay in close contact.'

'What do you mean by "close contact"?' asked the young man.

'There were two ways that he did it', explained Levy. 'First of all, he observed my activities very closely. He never seemed to be very far away. Secondly, he made me keep detailed records of my progress which he insisted I send to him.'

'That's interesting', said the young man. 'Why does he do that?'

'At first I thought he was spying and didn't trust me. That is, until I found out from some of the other people who report to him what he was really doing.'

'What was that?' the young man wanted to know.

'He was trying to catch me doing something right', Levy said.

'Catch you doing something right?' echoed the young man.

'Yes', replied Levy. 'We have a motto around here that says:

*Help People
Reach Their
Full Potential*

*Catch Them
Doing Something
Right*

Levy continued, 'In most organizations the managers spend most of their time catching people doing – what?' he asked the young man.

The young man smiled and said knowingly, 'Doing something wrong'.

'Right!' said Levy. 'Here we put the accent on the positive. We catch people doing something *right*.'

The young man made a few notes in his notebook and then asked, 'What happens, Mr. Levy, when the One Minute Manager catches you doing something right?'

'That's when he gives you a One Minute Praising', Levy said with a smile.

'What does that mean?' the young man wanted to know.

'Well, when he has seen that you have done something right, he comes over and makes contact with you. That often includes putting his hand on your shoulder or briefly touching you in a friendly way.'

'Doesn't it bother you when he touches you?' the young man wondered.

'No!' Levy insisted. 'On the contrary, it helps. I know he really cares about me and he wants me to prosper. As he says, "The more consistently successful your people are, the higher you rise in the organization".

'When he makes contact, it's brief, but it lets me know once again that we're really on the same side.

'Anyway, after that', Levy continued, 'he looks you straight in the eye and tells you precisely what you did right. Then he shares with you how good he feels about what you did.'

'I don't think I've ever heard of a manager doing that', the young man broke in. 'That must make you feel pretty good.'

The Second Secret: One Minute Praisings

'It certainly does', Levy confirmed, 'for several reasons. First of all, I get a praising as soon as I've done something right.' He smiled and leaned towards his visitor. Then he laughed and said, 'I don't have to wait for an annual performance review, if you know what I mean'. Both men smiled.

'Second, since he specifies exactly what I did right, I know he's sincere and familiar with what I am doing. Third, he is consistent.'

'Consistent?' echoed the young man, wanting to know more.

'Yes', insisted Levy. 'He will praise me if I am performing well and deserve it even if things are not going well for him elsewhere. I know he may be annoyed about other things. But he responds to my situation, not according to what's going on elsewhere for him at the time. And I really appreciate that.'

'Doesn't all this praising have to take up a lot of the manager's time?' the young man asked.

'Not really', said Levy. 'Remember you don't have to praise someone for very long for them to know you noticed and you care. It usually takes less than a minute.'

'And that's why it's called a One Minute Praising', the visitor said, as he wrote down what he was learning.

'Right', Levy said.

'Is he always trying to catch you doing something right?' the young man asked.

'No, of course not', Levy answered. 'Just when you first start work here or when you begin a new project or responsibility, then he does. After you get to know the ropes, he doesn't seem to be around much.'

'Why?' the young man wondered.

'Because you and he have other ways of knowing when your job performance is "praiseworthy". You both can review the data in the information system – the sales figures, expenditures, production schedules, and so on. And then', Levy added, 'after a while you begin to catch yourself doing things right and you start praising yourself. Also, you're always wondering when he might praise you again and that seems to keep you going even when he's not around. It's uncanny. I've never worked so hard at a job in my life.'

'That's really interesting', commented the young man. 'So One Minute Praising is a secret to becoming a One Minute Manager.'

'It is, indeed', Levy said with a gleam in his eye. He enjoyed watching someone learn the secrets of One Minute Management.

As the visitor looked at his notes, he quickly reviewed what he had learned about the One Minute Praising.

The One Minute Praising works well when you:

1. Tell people *right from the start* that you are going to let them know how they are doing.
2. Praise people immediately.
3. Tell people what they did right – be specific.
4. Tell people how good you feel about what they did right, and how it helps the organization and the other people who work there.
5. Stop for a moment of silence to let them *'feel'* how good you feel.
6. Encourage them to do more of the same.
7. Shake hands or touch people in a way that makes it clear that you support their success in the organization.

'What's the third secret?' the young man asked anxiously.

Levy laughed at the visitor's enthusiasm, rose from his chair and said, 'Why don't you ask Ms. Brown? I understand you're planning to talk to her, too.'

'Yes, I am', admitted the young man. 'Well, thanks so much for your time.'

'That's OK', insisted Levy. 'Time is one thing I have plenty of – you see, I'm a One Minute Manager myself now.'

The visitor smiled. He'd heard that somewhere before.

He wanted to reflect on what he was learning. He left the building and took a walk in a nearby park. He was struck again by the simplicity and common sense of what he had heard. 'You can't argue with the effectiveness of catching people doing something right', the young man thought, 'especially after they *know* what they are to do and what good performance looks like.

'But do One Minute Praisings really work?' he wondered. 'Does all this One Minute Management stuff really get results – bottom-line results?'

As he walked along his curiosity about results increased. So he returned to the One Minute Manager's secretary and asked Ms. Metcalfe to reschedule his appointment with Ms. Brown for some time the next morning.

'Tomorrow morning is fine', the secretary said as she put down the phone. 'Ms. Brown said to tell you to come any time except Wednesday morning.'

Then she rang another extension to make the new appointment he requested. He was to see Ms. Jones, an official at head office. 'They have information there about all the different plants and locations in the whole company', Ms. Metcalfe said in a very knowing way. 'I'm sure you'll find whatever you're looking for.' He thanked her and left.

AFTER lunch the young man went to his appointment at head office. There he met Ms. Jones, a competent looking woman in her early 40s. Getting down to business, the young man asked, 'Could you please tell me which of all your operations in the country is the most efficient and effective? I want to compare it with the so-called One Minute Manager's.'

A moment later, he laughed, as he heard Ms. Jones say, 'Well, you won't have to look very far, because it *is* the One Minute Manager's. He's quite a character, isn't he? His operation is the most efficient and effective of all of our plants.'

'That's unbelievable', said the young man. 'Does he have the best equipment?'

'No', said Ms. Jones. 'In fact, he's got some of the oldest.'

'Well, there's got to be something wrong there', said the young man, still puzzled by the old man's management style. 'Tell me, does he lose a lot of his people? Does he have a lot of turnover?'

'Come to think of it', Ms. Jones said, 'he does have a lot of turnover'.

'Aha', the young man said, thinking he was on to something.

'What happens to those people when they leave the One Minute Manager?' the young man wanted to know.

'We give them their own operation', Ms. Jones quickly responded. 'After two years with him, they say, "Who needs a manager?" He's our best trainer of people. Whenever we have an opening and need a good manager, we ring him. He always has somebody who is ready.'

Amazed, the young man thanked Ms. Jones for her time – but on this occasion he got a different response.

'I was glad I could fit you in today', she said. 'The rest of my week is really busy. I wish I knew what the One Minute Manager's secrets were. I've been meaning to go over there and see him, but I just haven't had time.'

Smiling, the young man said, 'I'll give you those secrets as a gift when I find them out myself. Just like he's giving them to me.'

'That would be a precious present', Ms. Jones said with a smile. She looked around her cluttered office and said, 'I could use whatever help I can get'.

The young man left Ms. Jones's office and walked out into the street, shaking his head. The One Minute Manager was absolutely fascinating to him.

That night the young man had a very restless sleep. He found himself excited about the next day – about learning the third secret to becoming a One Minute Manager.

THE next morning he arrived at Ms. Brown's office at the stroke of nine. A very smartly dressed woman in her late 50s greeted him. He got the usual, 'He's quite a character, isn't he?' routine, but by now the young man was getting to the point where he could sincerely say, 'Yes, he is!'

'Did he tell you about being a One Minute Manager?' asked Ms. Brown.

'That's all I've been hearing about', the young man said laughing. 'It's not true, is it?' he asked, still wondering if he'd get a different answer.

'You'd better believe it is. I hardly ever see him.'

'You mean you don't have much contact with him', pursued the young man, 'outside your regular weekly meeting?'

'Essentially very little. Except, of course, when I do something wrong', said Ms. Brown.

Shocked, the young man said, 'You mean the only time you see the One Minute Manager is when you do something wrong?'

'Yes. Well, not quite', said Ms. Brown, 'but almost'.

'But I thought a key motto around here was catching people doing things right.'

'It is', insisted Ms. Brown. 'But you have to know some things about me.'

'What?' asked the young man.

'I've been working here for quite a few years. I know this operation inside and out. As a result, the One Minute Manager doesn't have to spend much time with me, if any, on goal setting. In fact, I usually write out my goals and send them over to him.'

'Is each goal on a separate sheet of paper?' asked the young man.

'Indeed it is. No longer than 250 words and each one takes me or the One Minute Manager only a minute to read.

'Another thing about me that's important is that I just love my work. As a result, I do most of my own One Minute Praisings. In fact, I believe if you're not for yourself, who is? A friend of mine told me a motto I'll always remember: "If you don't blow your own horn, someone else will use it as a spittoon".'

The young man smiled. He liked her sense of humour. 'Does your manager ever praise you?' he asked.

'Sometimes he does, but he doesn't have to do it very often because I beat him to the punch', answered Ms. Brown. 'When I do something especially good, I might even ask the One Minute Manager for a praising.'

'How would you ever have the nerve to do that?' asked the young man.

'It's easy. Just like making a bet where I either win or I break even. If he gives me the praising, I win.'

'But if he doesn't?' the young man broke in.

'Then I break even', replied Ms. Brown. 'I didn't have it before I asked.'

The young man smiled as he took note of Ms. Brown's philosophy, and then continued.

'You said he spends time with you when you do something wrong. What do you mean?' asked the young man.

'If I make a significant mistake, that's when I invariably get a One Minute Reprimand', Ms. Brown said.

'A what?' the startled young man asked.

'A One Minute Reprimand', Ms. Brown repeated. 'That's the third secret to becoming a One Minute Manager.'

'How does it work?' wondered the young man out loud.

'It's simple', said Ms. Brown.

'I thought you'd say that', said the young man.

Ms. Brown joined his laugh and explained, 'If you have been doing a job for some time and you know how to do it well, and you make a mistake, the One Minute Manager is quick to respond'.

'What does he do?' asked the young man.

'As soon as he has learned about the mistake he comes to see me. First he confirms the facts. Then he might put his hand on my shoulder or maybe just come round to my side of the desk.'

'Doesn't that bother you?' asked the young man.

'Of course it does, because you know what's coming, especially since he doesn't have a smile on his face.

'He looks me straight in the eye', she continued, 'and tells me precisely what I did wrong. Then he shares with me how he feels about it – he's angry, annoyed, frustrated or whatever he is feeling.'

'How long does that take?' asked the young man.

'Only about 30 seconds but sometimes it seems forever to me', confided Ms. Brown.

The visitor couldn't help but remember how he himself felt when the One Minute Manager told him in no uncertain terms how annoyed he was with his indecision.

'And then what happens?' the young man asked as he moved to the edge of his chair.

'He lets what he said sink in with a few seconds of silence – and does it sink in!'

'Then what?' the young man asked.

'He looks me squarely in the eye and lets me know how competent he thinks I usually am. He makes sure I understand that the only reason he is angry with me is that he has so much respect for me. He says he knows this is so unlike me. He says how much he looks forward to seeing me some other time, as long as I understand that he does not welcome that same mistake again.'

The young man broke in. 'It must make you think twice.'

The Third Secret: One Minute Reprimands

'It certainly does', Ms. Brown nodded vigorously.

The young man knew what Ms. Brown was talking about. He was taking notes now as fast as he could. He sensed that it wasn't going to take this woman long to cover several important points.

'First of all', Ms. Brown said, 'he usually gives me the reprimand as soon as I've done something wrong. Second, since he specifies exactly what I did wrong, I know he is "on top of things" and that I'm not going to get away with sloppiness. Third, since he doesn't attack me as a person – only my behaviour – it's easier for me not to become defensive. I don't try to rationalize away my mistake by fixing blame on him or somebody else. I know he is being fair. And fourth, he is consistent.'

'Does that mean he will reprimand you for doing something wrong, even if things are going well for him elsewhere?'

'Yes', she answered.

'Does the whole process really take only a minute?' the young man asked.

'Usually', she said. 'And when it's over, it's over. A One Minute Reprimand doesn't last long but I can guarantee you, you don't forget it – and you don't usually make the same mistake twice.'

'I think I know what you're talking about', the young man said. 'I'm afraid I asked him. . . .'

'I hope', she interrupted, 'you didn't ask him to repeat himself'.

The young man was embarrassed. 'I did', he confessed.

'Then you know what it's like to be on the receiving end of a One Minute Reprimand', she said. 'Although I expect, as a visitor, you got a rather mild one.'

'I don't know if you'd call it mild', he said, 'but I don't think I'll ask him to repeat himself very often. That was a mistake.

'I wonder', the visitor continued, 'if the One Minute Manager ever makes a mistake. He seems almost too perfect.'

Ms. Brown began to laugh. 'Hardly', she said. 'But he does have a good sense of humour. So when he does make a mistake, like forgetting to do the last half of the One Minute Reprimand, we point it out to him and kid him about it.

'After we've had time to recover from the Reprimand, that is. We might, for example, phone him later and tell him we know we were wrong. Then we might laugh and ask for the praising half of the Reprimand, because we're not feeling too good.'

'And what does he do then?' the young man asked.

'He usually laughs and says he's sorry he forgot to remind me that I am OK as a person.'

'You can laugh about praisings and reprimands?' the young man asked.

'Of course', Ms. Brown said. 'You see, the One Minute Manager has taught us the value of being able to laugh at ourselves when we make a mistake. It helps us get on with our work.'

'That's terrific', the young man enthused. 'How did you learn to do that?'

'Simply', Ms. Brown answered, 'by watching the boss do it himself'.

'You mean your boss can laugh at himself when he makes a mistake?' the astonished young man asked.

'Well, not always', Ms. Brown admitted. 'He's like most of us. Sometimes it's tough. But he often can. And when he does laugh at himself, it has a positive effect on everyone around him.'

'He must be pretty secure', the young man suggested.

'He is', Ms. Brown answered.

The young man was impressed. He was beginning to see how valuable such a manager was to an organization.

'Why do you think the One Minute Manager's reprimands are so effective?' he asked.

'I'll let you ask the One Minute Manager', she said, as she rose from behind her desk and walked the young man to the door.

When he thanked her for her time, Ms. Brown smiled and said, 'You know what the response to that is going to be'. They both laughed. He was beginning to feel like an 'insider' rather than a visitor, and that felt good.

As soon as he was in the corridor, he realized how little time he'd spent with her and how much information she had given him.

He reflected on what she had said. It sounded so simple. He reviewed in his own mind what you should do when you catch an experienced person doing something wrong.

The One Minute Reprimand works well when you:

1. Tell people *beforehand* that you are going to let them know how they are doing and in no uncertain terms.

The first half of the reprimand:

2. Reprimand people immediately.
3. Tell people what they did wrong – be specific.
4. Tell people how you feel about what they did wrong – and in no uncertain terms.
5. Stop for a few seconds of uncomfortable silence to let them *feel* how you feel.

The second half of the reprimand:

6. Shake hands, or touch them in a way that lets them know you are honestly on their side.
7. Remind them how much you value them.
8. Reaffirm that you think well of them but not of their performance in this situation.
9. Realize that when the reprimand is over, it's over.

The young man would have found it hard to believe in the effectiveness of the One Minute Reprimand if he hadn't personally experienced its effect. There was no doubt that he felt uncomfortable. And he did not want to experience it again.

However, he knew that everyone made mistakes now and then, and that he might very well receive another reprimand some day. But he knew if it came from the One Minute Manager, that it would be fair; that it would be a comment on his behaviour and not on his worth as a person.

As he made his way to the One Minute Manager's office, he kept thinking about the simplicity of One Minute Management.

All three of the secrets made sense – One Minute Goals, One Minute Praisings, and One Minute Reprimands. 'But why do they work?' he wondered. 'Why is the One Minute Manager the most productive manager in the company?'

WHEN he got to the One Minute Manager's office, his secretary said, 'You can go straight in. He's been wondering when you'd be back to see him.'

As the young man entered the office, he noticed again how clear and uncluttered it was. He was greeted by a warm smile from the One Minute Manager.

'Well, what did you find out in your travels?' he asked.

'A lot!' the young man said enthusiastically.

'Tell me what you learned', the manager said encouragingly.

'I found out why you call yourself a One Minute Manager. You set One Minute Goals with your staff to make sure they know what they are being held accountable for and what good performance looks like. You then try to catch them doing something right so you can give them a One Minute Praising. And then, finally, if they have all the skills to do something right and they don't, you give them a One Minute Reprimand.'

'What do you think about all that?' asked the One Minute Manager.

'I'm amazed at how simple it is', said the young man, 'and yet it works – you get results. I'm convinced that it certainly works for you.'

'And it will for you too, if you're willing to *do* it', the manager insisted.

'Perhaps', said the young man, 'but I would be more likely to do it if I could understand more about *why* it works'.

'That's true of everyone, young man. The more you understand why it works, the more apt you are to *use* it. I'd be happy, therefore, to tell you what I know. Where do you want to start?'

'Well, first of all, when you talk about One Minute Management, do you really mean it takes a minute to do all the kinds of things you need to do as a manager?'

'No, not always. It is just a way to say that being a manager is not as complicated as people would have you believe. And also managing people doesn't take as long as you'd think. So when I say One Minute Management, it might take more than a minute for each of the key elements like goal setting, but it's just a symbolic term. And very often it does take only a minute.

'Let me show you one of the notes I keep on my desk.'

When he looked, the young man saw:

*

*The Best
Minute
I Spend
Is The One
I Invest
In People*

*

'It's ironic', the manager said. 'Most companies spend 50 per cent to 70 per cent of their money on people's salaries. And yet they spend less than 1 per cent of their budget to train their people. Most companies, in fact, spend more time and money on maintaining their buildings and equipment than they do on maintaining and developing people.'

'I never thought of that', the young man admitted. 'But if people get results, then it certainly makes good sense to invest in people.'

'Exactly', the manager said. 'I wish someone had invested in me sooner when I first went to work.'

'What do you mean?' the young man asked.

'Well, in most of the organizations I worked in before, I often didn't know what I was supposed to be doing. No one bothered to tell me. If you asked me whether I was doing a good job, I would say either "I don't know" or "I think so". If you asked why I thought so, I would reply, "I haven't been bawled out by my boss lately" or "No news is good news". It was almost as if my main motivation was to avoid punishment.'

'That's interesting', the young man admitted. 'But I'm not sure I understand it.'

Then he added anxiously, 'In fact, if it's all right with you, maybe I could understand things better if I could get to some of my "why" questions. Let's start with One Minute Goal Setting. Why does it work so well?'

'YOU want to know why One Minute Goals work', the manager said. 'Fine.' He got up and began to pace slowly around the room.

'Let me give you an analogy that might help. I've seen a lot of unmotivated people at work in the various organizations I've been employed by over the years. But I've never seen an unmotivated person after work. Everyone seems to be motivated to do something.

'One night, for example, I was bowling and I saw some of the "problem employees" at work from my last organization. One of the real problem people, whom I remembered all too well, took the bowling ball and approached the line and rolled the ball. Then he started to scream and yell and jump around. Why do you think he was so happy?'

'Because he got a strike. He had knocked down all the pins.'

'Exactly. Why don't you think he and other people are that excited at work?'

'Because he doesn't know where the pins are', smiled the young man. 'I get it. How long would he want to bowl if there were no pins?'

'Right', said the One Minute Manager. 'Now you can see what happens in most organizations. I believe that most managers know what they want their people to do. They just don't bother to tell their people in a way they would understand. They assume they should know. I never assume anything when it comes to goal setting.

'When you assume that people know what's expected of them, you are creating an ineffective form of bowling. You put the pins up but when the bowler goes to roll the ball, he notices there is a sheet across the pins. So when he rolls the ball, and it slips under the sheet, he hears a crack but doesn't know how many pins he's knocked down. When you ask him how he did, he says, *I don't know. But it felt good.*

'It's like playing golf at night. A lot of my friends have given up golf and when I asked them why, they said, "Because the courses are too crowded". When I suggested that they play at night, they laughed because who would ever play golf without being able to see the greens?

'It's the same with watching football. How many people in this country would sit in front of their television sets and watch two teams run up and down the field if there were no goals to shoot at or any way to score?"

'Yes! Why is that?' asked the young man.

'It's all because clearly the number one motivator of people is feedback on results. In fact, we have another saying here that's worth noting: *"Feedback is the Breakfast of Champions"*. Feedback keeps us going. Unfortunately, however, when most managers realize that feedback on results is the number one motivator of people, they usually set up a third form of bowling.

'When the bowler goes to the line to roll the ball, the pins are still up and the sheet is in place but now there is another ingredient in the game – a supervisor standing behind the sheet. When the bowler rolls the ball, he hears the crash of the falling pins, and the supervisor holds up two fingers to signify you knocked down two pins. Actually, do most managers say you got two?'

'No', the young man smiled. 'They usually say you missed eight.'

'Right!' said the One Minute Manager. 'The question I always used to ask was why the manager doesn't lift up the sheet so both he and his subordinate can see the pins. Why? Because he has the Annual Performance Review coming up.'

'Because he has Performance Review coming up?' wondered the young man.

'Yes. Such managers don't tell their people what they expect of them; they just leave them alone and then tear them off a strip when they don't perform at the desired level.'

'Why do you suppose they would do that?' the young man inquired, being very familiar with the truth in the manager's comments.

'So they can look good', said the manager.

'What do you mean, so they can look good?' asked the young man.

'How do you think you would be viewed by your boss if you rated everyone that reported to you at the highest level on your performance review scale?'

'As a "soft touch", as someone who could not discriminate between good performance and poor performance.'

'Precisely', said the manager. 'In order to look good as a manager in most organizations, you have to catch some of your people doing things wrong. You have to have a few winners, a few losers, and everyone else somewhere in the middle. You see, in this country we have a normal-distribution-curve mentality. I remember one time when visiting my son's school, I watched a teacher giving a geography test to her class. When I asked her why she didn't put atlases around the room and let the kids use them during the test, she said, "I couldn't do that because all the kids would get 100 per cent". As though it would be bad for everyone to do well.

'I remember once reading that when someone asked Einstein what his phone number was, he went to the phone book to look it up.'

The young man laughed. 'You're kidding.'

'No, I'm not kidding. He said he never cluttered his mind with information he could find somewhere else.

'Now, if you didn't know better', the manager continued, 'what would you think of someone who went to the phone book to look up his own number? Would you think he was a winner or a loser?'

The young man grinned and said, 'A real loser'.

'Of course you would', the manager said. 'I would, too, but we'd be wrong, wouldn't we?'

The young man nodded his agreement.

'It's easy for any of us to make this mistake', the manager said. Then he showed his visitor the plaque he had made for himself. 'Look at this':

*Everyone
Is A Potential Winner*

*Some People
Are Disguised
As Losers,*

*Don't Let
Their Appearances
Fool You*

*

'You see', the manager said, 'you really have three choices as a manager. First, you can hire winners. They are hard to find and they cost money. Or, second, if you can't find a winner, you can hire someone with the potential to be a winner. Then you systematically train that person to become a winner. If you are not willing to do either of the first two (and I am continually amazed at the number of managers who won't spend the money to hire a winner or take the time to train someone to become a winner), then there is only the third choice left – prayer.'

That stopped the young man cold. He put down his notebook and pen and said, 'Prayer?'

The manager laughed quietly. 'That's just my attempt at humour, young man. But when you think about it, there are many managers who are saying their prayers daily – "I hope this person works out".'

'Oh', the young man said seriously. 'Well, let's take the first choice. If you hire a winner, it's really easy to be a One Minute Manager, isn't it?'

'It certainly is', said the manager with a smile. He was amazed at how serious the young man was now – as though being more serious made a person a better manager. 'All you have to do with a winner is do One Minute Goal Setting and let them run with the ball.'

'I understand from Ms. Brown that sometimes you don't even have to do that with her', said the young man.

'She's absolutely right', said the manager. 'She's forgotten more than most people know around here. But with everyone, winner or potential winner, One Minute Goal Setting is a basic tool for productive behaviour.'

'Is it true that no matter who initiates the One Minute Goal Setting', the young man asked, 'each goal always has to be written down on a single sheet of paper?'

'Absolutely', insisted the One Minute Manager.

'Why is that so important?'

'So people can review their goals frequently and then check their performance against those goals.'

'I understand you insist they write down only their major goals and responsibilities and not every aspect of their job', the young man said.

'Yes. That's because I don't want this to be a paper mill. I don't want a lot of pieces of paper filed away somewhere and looked at only once a year when it's time for next year's goal setting or performance review, or some such thing.

'As you probably saw, everyone who works for me has a plaque near them that looks like this.' He showed his visitor his copy of the plaque.

*

Take A Minute:

Look At Your Goals

*Look At
Your Performance*

*See If Your Behaviour
Matches Your Goals*

*

The young man was amazed. He'd missed this in his brief visit. 'I never saw this', he said. 'It's terrific. Could I get one of these plaques?'

'Of course', the manager said. 'I'll arrange it.'

As he was writing down some of what he was learning, the aspiring manager said, without lifting up his head, 'You know, it's difficult to learn everything there is to learn about One Minute Management in such a short time. There's certainly more I'd like to learn about One Minute Goals, for instance, but maybe I could do that later.

'Could we move to One Minute Praisings now?' asked the young man, as he looked up from his notebook.

'Certainly', said the One Minute Manager. 'You're probably wondering why that works, too.'

'Indeed I am', the visitor responded.

'LET'S look at a few examples', the One Minute Manager said. 'Maybe then it will be clear to you why One Minute Praisings work so well.'

'I'd like that', said the young man.

'I'll start with a pigeon example and then move on to people', said the manager. 'Just remember, though, that people are not pigeons. People are more complicated. They are aware, they think for themselves and they certainly don't want to be manipulated by another person. Remember that and respect that. It is a key to good management.

'With that in mind, let us look at several simple examples which show us that we all seek what feels good to us and we avoid what feels bad to us.

'Suppose you have an untrained pigeon that you want to enter a box in the lower left-hand corner and run across the box to the upper right-hand corner and push a lever with his right foot. Suppose that not too far from the entry point we have a pellet machine – that is, a machine that can release pellets of food to reward and reinforce the pigeon. What do you think is going to happen if we put the pigeon in the box and wait until the pigeon runs over to the upper right-hand corner and pushes the lever with his right foot before we give him any food?' asked the One Minute Manager.

'He would starve to death', responded the young man.

'You're right. We're going to lose a lot of pigeons. The pigeon is going to starve to death because he has no idea what he is supposed to do.

'Now it's actually not too hard to train a pigeon to do this task. All you have to do is to draw a line not too far from where the pigeon enters the box. If the pigeon enters the box and crosses the line – bang – the pellet machine goes off and the pigeon gets fed. Pretty soon you have the pigeon running to that spot, but you don't want the pigeon there. Where do you want the pigeon?'

'In the upper right-hand corner of the box', said the young man.

'Right!' said the One Minute Manager. 'Therefore, after a while you stop rewarding the pigeon for running to that spot and draw another line which isn't too far from the last line, but is in the direction of the goal – the upper right-hand corner of the box. Now the pigeon starts running around his old spot and doesn't get fed. Pretty soon, though, the pigeon makes it across the new line and – bang – the machine goes off again and the pigeon gets fed.

'Then you draw another line. Again this line has to be in the direction of the goal, but not so far away that the pigeon can't make it again. We keep setting up these lines closer and closer to the upper right-hand corner of the box until we won't feed the pigeon unless he hits the lever, and then finally only when he hits the lever with his right foot.'

'Why do you set up all these little goals?' wondered the young man.

'By setting up these series of lines, we are establishing goals that the pigeon can achieve. So the key to training someone to do a new task is, in the beginning, to catch them doing something approximately right until they can eventually learn to do it exactly right.

'We use this concept all the time with kids and animals, but we somehow forget it when we are dealing with adults. For example, at some of these sea aquarium shows you see around the country, the show usually ends with a huge whale jumping over a rope which is high above the water. When the whale comes down he drenches the first ten rows.

'The people leave that show mumbling to themselves, "That's unbelievable. How do they teach that whale to do that?"

'Do you think they go out in the ocean in a boat', the manager asked, 'and put a rope out over the water and yell, "Up, up!" until a whale jumps out of the water over the rope? And then say, "Hey, let's hire him. He's a real winner".'

'No', laughed the young man, 'but that really *would* be hiring a winner'.

The two men enjoyed the laugh they shared.

'You're right', the manager said. 'When they captured the whale, he knew nothing about jumping over ropes. So when they began to train him in the large pool, where do you think they started the rope?'

'At the bottom of the pool', answered the young man.

'Of course!' retorted the manager. 'Every time the whale swam over the rope – which was every time he swam past – he got fed. Soon, they raised the rope a little.

'If the whale swam under the rope, he didn't get fed during training. Whenever he swam over the rope, he got fed. So after a while the whale started swimming over the rope all the time. Then they started raising the rope a little higher.'

'Why do they raise the rope?' asked the young man.

'First', the manager began, 'because they were clear on the goal: to get the whale to jump high out of the water and over the rope.

'And second', the One Minute Manager pointed out, 'it's not a very exciting show for a trainer to say, "Look, everyone, the whale did it again". Everybody may be looking in the water but they can't see anything. Over a period of time they keep on raising the rope until they finally get it to the surface of the water. Now the whale knows that, in order to get fed, he has to jump partially out of the water and over the rope. As soon as that goal is reached, they can start raising the rope higher and higher out of the water.'

'So that's how they do it', the young man said. 'Well, I can understand now how using that method works with animals, but isn't it a bit much to use it with people?'

'No, it's very natural, in fact', the manager said. 'We all do essentially the same thing with the children we care for. How do you think you teach them to walk? Can you imagine standing a child up and saying "Walk", and when he falls down you pick him up and spank him and say, "I told you to walk". No, you stand the child up and the first day he wobbles a little bit, and you get all excited and say, "He stood, he stood", and you hug and kiss the child. The next day he stands for a moment and maybe wobbles a step and you are all over him with kisses and hugs.

'Finally the child, realizing that this is a pretty good deal, starts to wobble his legs more and more until he eventually walks.

'The same thing goes for teaching a child to speak. Suppose you wanted a child to say, "Give me a glass of water, please". If you waited until the child said the whole sentence before you gave her any water, the child would die of thirst. So you start off by saying "Water, water". All of a sudden one day the child says, "Waller". You jump all over the place, hug and kiss the child, and get grandmother on the phone so the child can say "Waller, waller". That wasn't "water", of course, but it was close.

'Now you don't want a kid going into a restaurant at the age of twenty-one asking for a glass of "waller" so after a while you accept only the word "water" and then you begin on "please".

'These examples illustrate that the most important thing in training somebody to become a winner is to catch them doing something right – in the beginning approximately right and gradually moving them towards the desired behaviour. With a winner you don't have to catch them doing things right very often, because good performers catch themselves doing things right and are able to be self-reinforcing.'

'Is that why you observe new staff a lot in the beginning', asked the young man, 'or when your more experienced people are starting a new project?'

'Yes', the One Minute Manager said. 'Most managers wait until their staff do something exactly right before they praise them. As a result, many people never get to become high performers because their managers concentrate on catching them doing things wrong – that is, anything that falls short of the final desired performance. In our pigeon example, it would be like putting the pigeon in the box and not only waiting until he hits the lever to give him any food but putting some electric grilles around the box to punish him periodically just to keep him motivated.'

'That doesn't sound as though it would be very effective', the young man suggested.

'Well, it isn't', agreed the One Minute Manager. 'After getting punished for a while and not knowing what acceptable behaviour is (that is, hitting the lever), the pigeon would go into the corner of the box and not move. To the pigeon it is a hostile environment and not worth taking any risks in.

'That is what we often do with new, inexperienced people. We welcome them aboard, take them around to meet everybody, and then we leave them alone. Not only do we not catch them doing anything approximately right, but periodically we haul them over the coals just to keep them moving. This is the most popular leadership style of all. We call it the "leave alone–rebuke" style. You leave a person alone, expecting good performance from them, and when you don't get it, you rebuke them.'

'What happens to these people?' asked the young man.

'If you've been in any organization, and I understand you've visited several', the manager said, 'you know, because you've seen them. They do as little as possible.

'And that's what's wrong with most businesses today. Their people really do not produce – either quantity or quality.

'And much of the reason for this poor business performance is simply because the people are managed so poorly.'

The young man put down his notebook. He thought about what he just heard. He was beginning to see One Minute Management for what it is – a practical business tool.

It was amazing to him how well something as simple as the One Minute Praising worked – whether it was inside or outside the business world.

'That reminds me of some friends of mine', the young man said. 'They rang me and said that they'd bought a new dog. They asked me what I thought of their planned method for training the dog.'

The manager was almost afraid to ask, 'How were they going to do it?'

'They said if the dog had an accident on the carpet, they were going to take the dog, shove his nose in it, hit him with a newspaper and then throw him out of this little window in the kitchen into the garden – where the dog was supposed to do his job.

'Then, they asked me what I thought would happen with this method. I laughed because I knew what would happen. After about three days the dog would poop on the floor and jump out the window. The dog didn't know what to do, but he knew he had better clear the area.'

The manager roared his approval.

'That's a great story', he said. 'You see, that's what punishment does when you use it with somebody who lacks confidence or is insecure because of lack of experience. If inexperienced people don't perform (that is, do what you want them to do), then rather than punish them we need to go back to One Minute Goal Setting and make sure they understand what is expected of them, and that they have seen what good performance looks like.'

'Well, then, after you have done One Minute Goal Setting again', the young man asked, 'do you try to catch them doing something approximately right again?'

'Precisely so', the One Minute Manager agreed. 'You're always trying to create situations in the beginning where you can give a One Minute Praising.' Then, looking the young man straight in the eyes, the manager said, 'You are a very enthusiastic and receptive learner. That makes me pleased to be sharing the secrets of One Minute Management with you.' They both smiled. They knew a One Minute Praising when they heard one.

'I certainly prefer a praising to a reprimand', the young man laughed.

'I think I understand now why One Minute Goals and One Minute Praisings work. They really do make good sense to me.'

'Good', said the One Minute Manager.

'But I can't imagine why the One Minute Reprimand works', the young man wondered out loud.

'Let me tell you a few things about it', said the One Minute Manager.

'THERE are several reasons why the One Minute Reprimand works so well.

'To begin with', the manager explained, 'the feedback in the One Minute Reprimand is immediate. That is, you get to the individual as soon as you observe the "misbehaviour" or your data information system tips you off. It is not appropriate to save up negative feelings about someone's poor performance.

'The fact that the feedback is so immediate is an important lesson in why the One Minute Reprimand works so well. Unless discipline occurs as soon after the misbehaviour as possible, it tends not to be as helpful in influencing future behaviour. Most managers store up observations of poor behaviour and then some day when performance review comes or they are angry in general, they charge in and let fly with a long list of misdemeanours. They tell people all the things they have done wrong for the last few weeks or months or more.'

The young man breathed a deep sigh and said, 'So true'.

'And then', the One Minute Manager went on, 'the manager and subordinate usually end up yelling at each other about the facts or simply keeping quiet and resenting each other. The person receiving the feedback doesn't really hear what he or she has done wrong. This is a version of the "leave alone-rebuke" form of discipline that I've spoken about earlier.'

'I remember it well', responded the young man. 'That is certainly something I want to avoid.'

'Absolutely', agreed the manager. 'If managers would only intervene early, they could deal with one behaviour at a time and the person receiving the discipline would not be overwhelmed. They could hear the feedback. That's why I think performance review is an ongoing process, not something you do only once a year.'

'So, one reason that the One Minute Reprimand works is that the person receiving the reprimand can "hear" the feedback, because when the manager deals with one behaviour at a time, it seems more fair and clear', the young man summarized.

'Yes', the manager said. 'And secondly, when I give a One Minute Reprimand, I never attack a person's value as a person. Since their worth as a person is not on the line, they don't feel they have to defend themselves. I reprimand the *behaviour* only. Thus, my feedback and their own reaction to it is about the specific behaviour and not their feelings about themselves as human beings.

'So often, when disciplining people, managers persecute the individual. My purpose in a One Minute Reprimand is to eliminate the behaviour and keep the person.'

'So that's why you make the second half of the reprimand a praising', the young man said. 'Their behaviour is not all right. They are all right.'

'Yes', agreed the One Minute Manager.

'Why wouldn't you give the praising first and then the reprimand?' suggested the young man.

'For some reason, it just doesn't work', insisted the manager. 'Some people, now that I think of it, say that I am nice and tough as a manager. But to be more accurate, I'm really tough and nice.'

'Tough and nice', echoed the young man.

'Yes', insisted the One Minute Manager. 'This is an old philosophy that has worked well for literally thousands of years.

'There is, in fact, a story in ancient China that illustrates this. Once upon a time, an emperor appointed a second in command. He called this prime minister in and, in effect, said to him, *Why don't we divide up the tasks? Why don't you do all the punishing and I'll do all the rewarding?* The prime minister said, *Fine. I'll do all the punishing and you do all the rewarding.*'

'I think I'm going to like this story', the young man said.

'You will, you will', the One Minute Manager replied with a knowing smile.

'Now this emperor', the manager continued, 'soon noticed that whenever he asked someone to do something, they might do it or they might not do it. However, when the prime minister spoke, people moved. So the emperor called in the prime minister again and said, *Why don't we divide the tasks again? You have been doing all the punishing here for quite a while. Now let me do the punishing and you do the rewarding.* So the prime minister and the emperor switched roles again.

'And, within a month, the prime minister was emperor. The emperor had been a nice person, rewarding and being kind to everyone; then he started to punish people. People said, *What's wrong with that old codger?* and they threw him out on his ear. When they came to look for a replacement, they said, *You know who's really starting to come around now – the prime minister.* So they put him into office.'

'Is that a true story?' the young man asked.

'Who cares?' said the One Minute Manager, laughing. 'Seriously', he added, 'I do know this. If you are first tough on the behaviour, and *then* supportive of the person, it works.'

'Do you have any modern-day examples of where the One Minute Reprimand has worked other than in management?' the young man asked the manager.

'Yes, certainly', the manager said. 'Let me mention two: one with severe adult behaviour problems and another in disciplining children.'

'What do you mean when you say "severe adult behaviour problems"?' the young man asked.

'I'm talking about alcoholics in particular', the manager answered. 'About thirty years ago an observant clergyman discovered a technique which is now called "crisis intervention". He made the discovery when he was helping a physician's wife. She had been taken to hospital in a critical condition and was slowly dying from cirrhosis of the liver. But she was still denying that she had a drinking problem. When all her family had gathered at her bedside, the clergyman asked each of them to describe specific drinking incidents they had observed. That's an important part of the One Minute Reprimand. Before giving a reprimand you have to see the behaviour yourself – you can't depend on what someone else saw. You never give a reprimand based on hearsay.'

'Interesting', the young man broke in.

'Let me finish. After the family described specific behaviours, the clergyman asked each of the family members to tell the woman how they felt about those incidents. Gathered closely around her, one by one they told her first what she *did*, and second, how they *felt* about it. They were angry, frustrated, embarrassed. And then they told her how much they loved her, and they instinctively touched her and gently said how they wanted her to live and to enjoy life once again. That was why they were so angry with her.'

'That sounds so simple', said the young man, 'especially with something as complicated as a drinking problem. Did it work?'

'Amazingly so', the One Minute Manager insisted. 'It's not as simple as I've summarized it, of course. But these three basic ingredients – telling people what they did wrong; telling people how you feel about it; and reminding people that they are valuable and worthwhile – lead to significant improvements in people's behaviour.'

'That's nothing short of incredible', the young man said.

'I know it is', the manager agreed.

'You said you'd give me two examples of how other people successfully use methods like the One Minute Reprimand', the young man said.

'Yes, of course. In the early 1970s, a family psychiatrist in California also made the same amazing discovery with children. He had read a lot about bonding – the emotional ties people have to people. He knew what people needed. People need to be in contact with people who care about them – to be accepted as valuable just because they are people.

'The doctor also knew that people need to have a spade called a spade – to be pulled up short by people who care when they are not behaving well.'

'How does that translate', the young man wanted to know, 'into practical action?'

'Each parent is taught to physically touch their child by putting their hand on the child's shoulder, touching his arm or, if he is young, actually sitting the child on their lap. Then the parent tells the child exactly what he did wrong and how the parent feels about it – and in no uncertain terms. (You can see that this is very like what the family members did for the sick woman.) Finally, the parent takes a deep breath, and allows for a few seconds of silence – so the child can *feel* whatever the parent is feeling. Then the parent tells the youngster how valuable and important the child is to the parent.

'You see, it is very important when you are managing people to remember that behaviour and worth are not the same things. What is really worthwhile is the *person* managing their own behaviour. This is as true of each of us as managers as it is of each of the people we are managing.

'In fact, if you know this', the manager said, as he pointed to one of his favourite plaques, 'you will know the key to a really successful reprimand'.

*We Are Not
Just
Our Behaviour*

*We Are
The Person
Managing
Our Behaviour*

'If you realize that you are managing people, and not just their recent behaviour', the manager concluded, 'you will do well'.

'It sounds as though there's a lot of caring and respect behind such a reprimand', the young man said.

'I'm glad you noticed that, young man. You will be successful with the One Minute Reprimand when you really care about the welfare of the person you are reprimanding.'

'That reminds me', the young man said, 'Mr. Levy told me that you pat him on the shoulder, or shake hands, or in some other way make contact with him during a praising. And now I notice that the parents are encouraged to touch their children during the scolding. Is touching an important part of the One Minute Praisings and Reprimands?'

'Yes and no', the manager answered with a smile. 'Yes, if you know the person well and are clearly interested in helping the person to succeed in his or her work. And no, if you or the other person has any doubts about that.

'Touch is a very powerful message', the manager pointed out. 'People have strong feelings about being touched, and that needs to be respected. Would you, for instance, like someone whose motives you weren't sure of to touch you during a praising or a reprimand?'

'No', the young man answered clearly. 'I really wouldn't!'

'You see what I mean', the manager explained. 'Touch is very honest. People know immediately when you touch them whether you care about them, or whether you are just trying to find a new way to manipulate them.

'There is a very simple rule about touching', the manager continued. *'When you touch, don't take.* Touch the people you manage only when you are *giving* them something – reassurance, support, encouragement, or whatever.'

'So you should refrain from touching someone', the young man said, 'until you know them and they know you are interested in their success – that you are clearly on their side. I can see that.

'But', the young man continued hesitantly, 'while the One Minute Praisings and the One Minute Reprimands look simple enough, aren't they really just powerful ways for you to get people to do what you want them to do? And isn't that manipulative?'

'You are right about One Minute Management being a powerful way to get people to do what you want them to do', the manager confirmed.

'However, manipulation is getting people to do something they are either *not aware of* or *don't agree to*. That is why it is so important to let each person know *right from the start* what you are doing and why.

'It's like anything else in life', the manager explained. 'There are things that work, and things that don't work. Being honest with people eventually works. On the other hand, as you have probably learned in your own life, being dishonest eventually leads to failing with people. It's just that simple.'

'I can see now', the young man said, 'where the power of your management style comes from – you care about people'.

'Yes', the manager said simply, 'I do'.

The young man remembered how gruff he thought this special manager was when he first met him.

It was as though the manager could read his mind.

'Sometimes', the One Minute Manager said, 'you have to care enough to be tough. And I am. I am very tough on the poor performance – but only on the performance. I am never tough on the person.'

The young man liked the One Minute Manager. He knew now why people liked to work with him.

'Maybe you would find this interesting', the younger man said, as he pointed to his notebook. 'It is a plaque I've created to remind me of how *goals* – the One Minute Goals – and *consequences* – the Praisings and the Reprimands – affect people's behaviour.'

*Goals
Begin
Behaviours*

*Consequences
Maintain
Behaviours*

*

'That's very good!' the manager exclaimed.

'Do you think so?' the young man asked, wanting to hear the compliment once again.

'Young man', the manager said very slowly for emphasis, 'it is not my role in life to be a human tape recorder. I do not have time to continually repeat myself.'

Just when he thought he would be praised, the young man felt he was in for another One Minute Reprimand, something he wanted to avoid.

The bright young man kept a straight face and said simply, 'What did you say?'

They looked at each other only for a moment and then they both started to laugh.

'I like you, young man', the manager said. 'How would you like to go to work here?'

The young man put down his notebook and stared in amazement. 'You mean go to work for you?' he asked enthusiastically.

'No. I mean go to work for yourself like the other people in my department. Nobody ever really works for anybody else. I just help people work better and in the process they benefit our organization.'

This was, of course, what the young man had been looking for all along.

'I'd love to work here', he said.

And so he did – for some time.

The time the special manager had invested in him paid off. Because eventually, the inevitable happened.

He became a One Minute Manager.

He became a One Minute Manager not because he thought like one, or talked like one, but because he behaved like one.

He set One Minute Goals.

He gave One Minute Praisings.

He gave One Minute Reprimands.

He asked brief, important questions; spoke the simple truth; laughed, worked, and enjoyed.

And, perhaps most important of all, he encouraged the people he worked with to do the same.

He had even created a pocket-sized 'Game Plan' to make it easier for the people around him to become One Minute Managers. He had given it as a useful gift to each person who reported to him.

A very brief summary of
THE ONE MINUTE MANAGER'S "GAME PLAN"
How to give yourself & others 'the gift' of getting greater results in less time.
SET GOALS; PRAISE & REPRIMAND BEHAVIOURS; ENCOURAGE PEOPLE;
SPEAK THE TRUTH; LAUGH; WORK; ENJOY
and encourage the people you work with to do the same as you do!

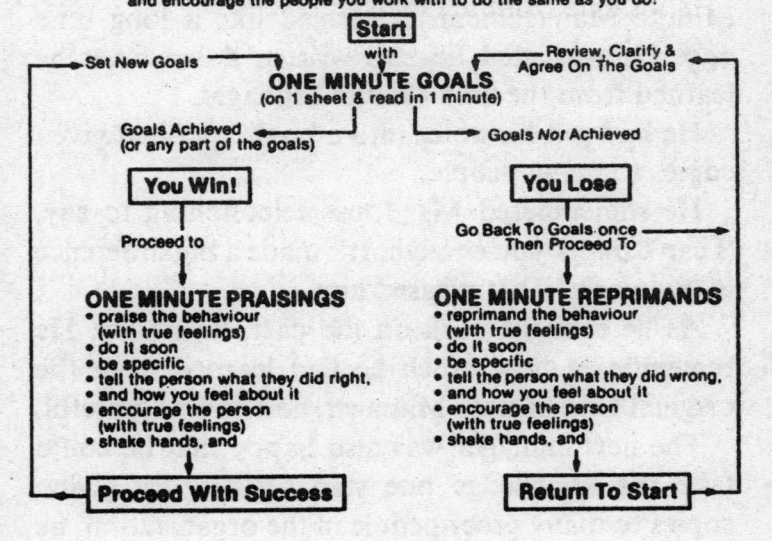

Start
with

← Set New Goals   **ONE MINUTE GOALS**   Review, Clarify & →
                       (on 1 sheet & read in 1 minute)   Agree On The Goals

Goals Achieved ←   → Goals *Not* Achieved
(or any part of the goals)

You Win!   **You Lose**

Proceed to   Go Back To Goals once →
                                              Then Proceed To

ONE MINUTE PRAISINGS   **ONE MINUTE REPRIMANDS**
• praise the behaviour   • reprimand the behaviour
  (with true feelings)   (with true feelings)
• do it soon   • do it soon
• be specific   • be specific
• tell the person what they did right,   • tell the person what they did wrong,
• and how you feel about it   • and how you feel about it
• encourage the person   • encourage the person
  (with true feelings)   (with true feelings)
• shake hands, and   • shake hands, and

Proceed With Success   **Return To Start**

MANY years later, the man looked back on the time when he first heard of the principles of One Minute Management. It seemed like a long time ago. He was glad he had written down what he learned from the One Minute Manager.

He had put his notes into a book, and had given copies to many people.

He remembered Ms. Jones telephoning to say, 'I can't thank you enough. It's made a big difference in my work.' That pleased him.

As he thought back on the past, he smiled. He remembered how much he had learned from the original One Minute Manager, and he was grateful.

The new manager was also happy that he could take the knowledge one step further. By giving copies to many other people in the organization, he had solved several practical problems.

Everyone who worked with him felt secure. No one felt manipulated or threatened because everyone knew right from the start what he was doing and why.

They could also see *why* the seemingly simple One Minute Management techniques - Goals, Praising and Reprimands - worked so well with people.

Every person who had their own copy of the text could read and re-read it at their own pace until they could understand it and put it to good use themselves. The manager knew full well the very practical advantage of repetition in learning anything new.

Sharing the knowledge in this simple and honest way had, of course, saved him a good deal of time. And it had certainly made his job easier.

Many of the people reporting to him had become One Minute Managers themselves. And they, in turn, had done the same for many of the people who reported to them.

The entire organization had become more effective.

As he sat at his desk thinking, the new One Minute Manager realized what a fortunate individual he was. He had given himself the gift of getting greater results in less time.

He had time to think and to plan – to give his organization the kind of help it needed.

He had time to exercise and stay healthy.

He knew he did not experience the daily emotional and physical stress other managers subjected themselves to.

And he knew that many of the other people who worked with him enjoyed the same benefits.

His department had fewer costly personnel turnovers, less personal illness, and less absenteeism. The benefits were significant.

Then he got up from his desk and began to walk about his uncluttered office. He was deep in thought.

He felt good about himself – as a person and as a manager.

His caring about people had paid off handsomely. He had risen in the organization, gaining more responsibilities and more rewards.

And he knew he had become an effective manager, because both his organization and the people in it had clearly benefited from his presence.

106 / A Gift For Others

SUDDENLY the intercom buzzed and startled the man. 'Excuse me for interrupting you', he heard his secretary say, 'but there is a young woman on the phone. She wants to know if she can come and talk to you about the way we manage people here.'

The new One Minute Manager was pleased. He knew more women were entering the business world. And he was glad that some of them were as keen to learn about good management as he had been.

The manager's department was now running smoothly. As you might expect, it was one of the best operations of its kind in the world. The members of his staff were productive and happy. And he was happy too. It felt good to be in his position.

'Come any time', he heard himself telling the caller.

And soon he found himself talking to a bright young person. 'I'm glad to share my management secrets with you', the new One Minute Manager said, as he showed the visitor to a seat. 'I will only make one request of you.'

'What's that?' the visitor asked.

'Simply', the manager began, 'that you:'

*

Share It With Others

*

Acknowledgments

Over the years we have learned from, and been influenced by, many individuals. We would like to acknowledge and give a public praising to the following people:

A Special Praising to:

**Dr. Gerald Nelson*, the originator of The One Minute Scolding, an amazingly effective method of parental discipline. We have adapted his method into 'The One Minute Reprimand', an equally effective method of *managerial* discipline. Dr. Nelson is also co-author of *The One Minute Scolding*.

and to:

Dr. Elliott Carlisle for what he taught us about productive managers who have time to think and plan.

Dr. Thomas Connellan for what he taught us about making behavioural concepts and theories clear and understandable to all.

Dr. Paul Hersey for what he taught us about weaving the various applied behavioural sciences into a useful fabric.

Dr. Vernon Johnson for what he taught us about the Crisis Intervention Method of treatment for alcoholics.

Dr. Dorothy Jongeward, *Jay Shelov*, and *Abe Wagner* for what they taught us about communication and the worth of people *as* people.

Dr. Robert Lorber for what he taught us about the application and use of behavioural concepts in business and industry.

Dr. Kenneth Majer for what he taught us about goal-setting and performance.

Dr. Charles McCormick for what he taught us about touching and professionalism.

Dr. Carl Rogers for what he taught us about personal honesty and openness.

Louis Tice for what he taught us about unlocking human potential.

About the Authors

Dr. Kenneth Blanchard, President of Blanchard Training and Development, Inc. (BTD), is an internationally known author, educator and consultant/trainer. He is the co-author of the highly acclaimed and most widely used text on leadership and organization behaviour, *Management of Organization Behaviour: Utilizing Human Resources*, which is in its fourth edition and has been translated into numerous languages.

Dr. Blanchard received his B.A. from Cornell University in Government and Philosophy, an M.A. from Colgate University in Sociology and Counselling and a Ph.D. from Cornell in Administration and Management. He presently serves as a professor of Leadership and Organizational Behaviour at University of Massachusetts, Amherst. In addition, he is a member of the National Training Laboratories (NTL).

Dr. Blanchard has advised such distinguished corporations and agencies as Chevron, Lockheed, AT&T, Holiday Inns, Young Presidents' Organization, the United States Armed Forces, and UNESCO. The Hersey/Blanchard Situational Leadership approach to management has been incorporated into the training and development programmes of Mobil Oil, Caterpillar, Union 76, IBM, Xerox, The Southland Corporation, and numerous fast-growing entrepreneurial companies. In his role as management consultant, Dr. Blanchard teaches seminars throughout America. He is president of Blanchard Training and Development, Inc., in Escondido, California.

Dr. Spencer Johnson is the Chairman of Candle Communications Corporation, and an active author, publisher, lecturer and communications consultant. He has written more than a dozen books dealing with medicine and psychology, and has over three million copies of his books in print.

Dr. Johnson's education includes a degree in psychology from the University of Southern California, an M.D. degree from the Royal College of Surgeons in Ireland, and medical clerkships at Harvard Medical School and the Mayo Clinic.

He has been Medical Director of Communications for Medtronic, a pioneering manufacturer of cardiac pacemakers, and Research Physician for the Institute For Interdisciplinary Studies, a medical-social think-tank in Minneapolis. He has also served as a consultant in communications for the Centre for the Study of the Person, Human Dimensions in Medicine Programme; and to the Office of Continuing Education at the School of Medicine, University of California in La Jolla, California.

One of his recent books, *The Precious Present*, has been praised by the eminent psychologist Dr. Carl Rogers, and by Dr. Norman Vincent Peale, who states, 'What a change might take place if everyone would read this book and apply the principles it teaches'.

The One Minute Manager, like all the other books Dr. Johnson has written, reflects his continuing interest in helping people to experience less stress and better health through better communications. Dr. Johnson and Dr. Blanchard have also produced, in conjunction with 20th Century-Fox, *The One Minute Manager* videotape.

Putting The One Minute Manager to Work

How to turn the 3 Secrets into Skills

Kenneth Blanchard, Ph.D.
Robert Lorber, Ph.D.

:01 *The Symbol*

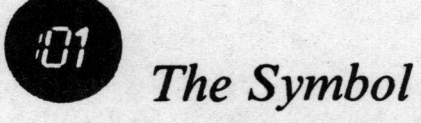

The One Minute Manager's symbol –
a one minute readout from the face of
a modern digital watch – is intended to
remind each of us to take a minute out
of our day to look into the faces of the
people we manage. And to realise that
they are our most important resources.

Contents

The Question *9*
The One Minute Manager *10*
Easier Said Than Done *14*
The ABC's of Management *18*
A Basic Course in ABC's *21*
The ABC's of Management: A Summary *22*
Managing Winners *37*
Effective Reprimanding *39*
Theory into Practice *47*
Setting the Stage for PRICE *50*
The PRICE System *53*
Pinpoint the Performance *54*
Record Current Performance *55*
Involve People *58*
Coach for Performance *67*
Evaluate Progress *70*
The PRICE System: A Summary *76*
Chris Pays the PRICE *77*
Some Final Thoughts *89*
Making a Commitment *90*
Putting the One Minute Manager to Work *91*

About the Authors *94*
Concept Praisings *96*

TO

Our wives, Margie and Sandy,
for their constant love
and support throughout
the highs and lows
of our lives

01 Introduction

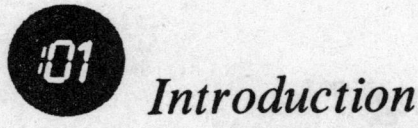

In the last episode of *The One Minute Manager*, the bright young man who was searching for an effective manager learned the One Minute Manager's three secrets. He immediately realised that they were the key to effective management.

The young man learned the One Minute secrets well, because eventually the inevitable happened: he became a One Minute Manager.

He set One Minute Goals.

He gave One Minute Praisings.

He delivered One Minute Reprimands.

In this second episode of *The One Minute Manager*, a veteran manager wonders whether using the three secrets on a day-to-day basis will really make a difference where it counts – in performance. Bothered by this question, he seeks the answer from a new One Minute Manager. In the process he learns how to put the One Minute Manager to work in a systematic way to achieve excellence.

This book is meant to be a companion to the original book. It is a practical tool that can be used independently to implement the three secrets of the One Minute Manager but will probably be a richer experience if you have first read *The One Minute Manager*.

We hope you apply and use what the veteran manager learns and see if it doesn't make a difference in your life and the lives of those who work with you.

Kenneth Blanchard, Ph.D.
Robert Lorber, Ph.D.

01 Putting The One Minute Manager To Work

WHEN the veteran manager finished reading *The One Minute Manager*, he put the book down on his coffee table. He leaned back with a questioning look. He had first read the book at the office but had brought it home to give it another reading.

'Even after a second time through', he thought to himself, 'I cannot argue with the logic of the three secrets of the One Minute Manager. But if I practise them, will I actually become a more productive manager?'

The veteran manager decided to do something about his question. The next morning he would telephone a manager in a town some distance away who had, in recent years, turned a troublesome company into a very profitable enterprise. The veteran had read a newspaper interview with this manager in which he had credited much of his success to practising One Minute Management. In fact, he now called himself a 'One Minute Manager'.

THE next morning when the veteran manager got to his office, he rang the new One Minute Manager. He introduced himself and asked the manager if he could see him at some time that week and talk about One Minute Management. The veteran had been warned what the answer might be but he was still surprised when the One Minute Manager actually said, 'Come any time except Wednesday morning. That's when I meet with my key staff. To be honest with you, I don't have much scheduled this week. I'll be glad to talk to you.'

'I'll be there tomorrow morning at ten', said the veteran manager, chuckling to himself. When he put down the phone he thought, 'This ought to be interesting. I'm sure I'll get my questions answered.'

When the veteran manager arrived at the One Minute Manager's office, the secretary said, 'He's expecting you. Go straight in.'

As he entered the room, he found a man in his late forties standing by the window looking out.

The veteran manager coughed and the One Minute Manager looked up. He smiled and said, 'Good to see you. Let's sit down over here.' He led the manager to a pair of comfortable chairs in the corner of the room.

'Well, what can I do for you?' the One Minute Manager asked as he sat down.

'I have read *The One Minute Manager* and so have my staff', the veteran manager began. 'I'm enthusiastic about it and so are they, but that has happened before when a new management system has been introduced. My question is how do you put One Minute Management to work in a way that turns the secrets into usable skills and makes a difference where it really counts – in performance?'

'Before I attempt to answer that question', said the One Minute Manager, 'let me ask you one. What do you think the message of One Minute Management is?'

'It's quite simple', said the veteran manager. 'If you have a sheet of paper I'll write it down for you.'

The One Minute Manager went over to his desk and got a pad. He gave it to the veteran manager. Without pausing the veteran manager wrote:

*People Who Produce
Good Results*

*Feel Good
About Themselves*

*

'That's an interesting twist', said the One Minute Manager, gesturing to a plaque on the wall behind his desk. It read: *"People Who Feel Good About Themselves Produce Good Results"*. 'Why did you change it?' he asked.

'I think it represents more accurately the essence of One Minute Management', insisted the veteran manager, 'and besides, it's more consistent with what you teach'.

'Consistent?' questioned the One Minute Manager.

'Yes', responded the veteran manager firmly. 'You say that one of the key ingredients to a One Minute Praising is to be specific – to tell the person exactly what he or she did right.'

'That's true', said the One Minute Manager.

'Then praisings, which help make people feel good about themselves, are not effective unless those people have done something positive first', smiled the veteran manager, feeling he had the One Minute Manager trapped.

'You're a tough man', laughed the One Minute Manager, 'and you really have a good idea about what One Minute Management is all about. I think I can learn a few things from you. I'll feel good about sharing as much as I can with you.'

'I doubt if you will learn much from me', said the veteran manager. 'I'm just a "street fighter" who has survived.'

'Can't take a compliment, is that it?' mused the One Minute Manager. 'Most people can't quite accept being praised.'

'I would imagine that's because we've never had much practice receiving praisings', said the veteran manager. 'And it's not easy to do something that you're not used to doing, even if you believe in it.'

'Right', said the One Minute Manager. 'One of the reasons it's hard to implement One Minute Management is that people will have to change some of their old behaviour. And focusing on and changing how people treat each other in organisations is something that only gets lip service. Most top managers think that management training is just a fringe benefit – a nice little frill they can give all their employees every year. That's why I have that saying on the wall', he said as he gestured to a plaque on the other side of the room. It said:

*

*Most Companies
Spend All Their Time
Looking For Another
Management Concept
And
Very Little Time
Following Up The One
They Have Just Taught
Their Managers*

*

'That's so true', said the veteran manager. 'And people do the same thing. They're always looking for the next "quick fix" rather than using what they have already learned. They go from one diet programme to another diet programme, one exercise plan to another without following the last plan.'

'Then they wonder why they don't lose weight or build up their heart', said the One Minute Manager. 'It reminds me of a story of the man who slipped and fell off a cliff while hiking on a mountaintop. Luckily he was able to grab a branch on his way down. Holding on for dear life, he looked down to see a rock valley some fifteen hundred feet below. When he looked up it was twenty feet to the cliff where he had fallen.

'Panicked, he yelled, "Help! Help! Is anybody up there? Help!"

'A booming voice spoke up. "I am here and I will save you if you believe in me".

'"I believe! I believe!" yelled back the man.

'"If you believe in me", said the voice, "let go of the branch and then I will save you".

'The young man, hearing what the voice said, looked down again. Seeing the rock valley below, he quickly looked back up and shouted, "Is there anybody else up there?"'

'That's a good one', laughed the veteran manager. 'That's exactly what I don't want to do – hold onto the branch and keep looking for another system. One Minute Management is the way I want to manage and be managed. All I want to know is how to put it to work so that it lasts and makes a difference.'

'Then you came to the right place', said the One Minute Manager. 'What problems have you been having using the three secrets?'

'I think the main difficulty I have experienced', said the veteran manager, 'has been turning the secrets into skills. That is, knowing when to do what. For example, sometimes I think I'm reprimanding when I should be goal setting and at other times I'm goal setting when I should be reprimanding.'

'I had the same trouble', said the One Minute Manager, 'until I learned my ABC's'.

'I know you're not talking about the ABC's of school days', said the veteran. 'So what do you mean?'

'NO, I'm not referring to the alphabet, but the ABC's are a way of getting back to basics. They've helped this organisation make the transition from secrets to skills. We knew the three secrets of One Minute Management, and we were really enthusiastic, but they weren't working for us in day-to-day performance until we learned the ABC's of management', said the One Minute Manager. Picking up his notepad he wrote:

> A = Activators
> B = Behaviour
> C = Consequences

Then he began his explanation:

'*A* stands for *activators*. Activators are those things that have to be done by a manager before someone can be expected to accomplish a goal. *B* stands for *behaviour* or performance. It is what a person says or does. *C* stands for *consequences* or what a manager does after someone accomplishes or attempts to accomplish a goal. If managers can learn to understand and deliver the necessary activators (A) and consequences (C), they can ensure more productive behaviour (B) or performance.'

'So learning your ABC's is a key to performance', said the veteran.

'It certainly is', said the One Minute Manager. 'A number of companies throughout the country have realised that they can experience significant performance improvement by following up and getting their managers to actually use the ABC's and other implementation strategies I'll teach you. And what's interesting about these companies is that they are from a variety of businesses and industries – banking and finance, construction, communication, energy utilisation, high technology, hotels and restaurants, and retail merchandising. And they worked on all kinds of performance areas including productivity (both quality and quantity), safety, staff retention, sales, costs and profits. In every case real "bottom line" improvements were experienced.'

'You've got my interest', said the veteran manager. 'I think I'd better learn more about the ABC's if I want to put One Minute Management to work and make those kinds of differences.'

'Why don't you go and see one of my staff, Tom Connelly', said the One Minute Manager. 'He took over a work group that averaged nearly a 50 per cent annual staff turnover. Now it's down to less than ten per cent. He can tell you all about the ABC's.'

'I'd love to meet him', said the veteran manager. 'But before you ring him, let me ask you one more thing. Do you always talk in threes? First three secrets and now ABC's.'

'Not always', smiled the One Minute Manager. 'But I believe in the KISS method: "Keep it short and simple". I don't think people can remember a whole lot of things, particularly if they are going to use what they have learned.'

'Isn't KISS usually "Keep it Simple Stupid"?' wondered the veteran manager.

'Yes', admitted the One Minute Manager. 'But since One Minute Management is a positive approach to managing people, we use a positive way to express the concept.'

'I knew you'd have a good explanation', smiled the veteran. 'I'm looking forward to meeting Connelly.'

The One Minute Manager dialled a number and said, 'Tom, I have an experienced manager here who wants to learn his ABC's. Are you free?'

Although the veteran could not hear everything clearly, he smiled as he thought he heard Connelly say, 'Send him over. I've just got back. I was out having fun catching my people doing things right.'

'Come back and see me when you've finished talking to Tom', said the One Minute Manager as he led the veteran manager to the door.

'Certainly', said the veteran manager. 'Thanks for your time.'

WHEN the veteran manager got to Connelly's office, he found a smartly dressed man in his mid-forties.

As Connelly got up from his desk and introduced himself, the veteran manager got right to the point: 'Your boss told me you could give me the real low down on the ABC's of management'.

'I'll try', said Connelly. 'Let me start off by giving you this summary that we use so everyone can remember their ABC's.' He handed the veteran manager a chart.

THE ABC's OF MANAGEMENT: A Summary

The term:

A	B	C
ACTIVATOR	BEHAVIOUR	CONSEQUENCE

What it means:

What a manager does *before* performance	Performance: What someone says or does	What a manager does *after* performance

Examples:

One Minute Goal Setting ● Areas of accountability ● Performance standards ● Instructions	● Writes report ● Sells shirt ● Comes to work ● Misses deadline ● Types letter ● Makes mistake ● Fills order	*One Minute Praising* ● Immediate, specific ● Shares feelings *One Minute Reprimand* ● Immediate, specific ● Shares feelings ● Supports individual *No response*

The veteran manager read the chart very carefully. When he finished reading he looked up, smiled and said, 'So One Minute Goal Setting is an activator?'

'Yes', said Connelly. 'An activator is like an "ante" in poker. It gets things started.'

'If goal setting is an activator', said the veteran, 'then you're not in the management game unless your staff are clear on their key areas of responsibility (accountability) and what good performance in each of those areas looks like (performance standards)'.

'That's why goal setting is the most important activator for managers to remember', said Connelly. 'It starts the whole management process.'

'Sounds good', affirmed the veteran manager. 'Once people are activated, then they are ready to perform.'

'They certainly are', said Connelly. 'It's that performance that managers need to watch. Once you have asked someone to do something, what they say or do while trying to accomplish the desired task is their performance or behaviour – the *B* of ABC's.'

'Is what people think or feel considered to be behaviour?' asked the veteran manager.

'No', said Connelly. 'While thoughts and feelings are important since they often determine what people do, they are not considered behaviour because they are behind the eyeballs.'

'In other words', jumped in the veteran, 'you cannot see them'.

'Right', said Connelly. 'Once you get into thoughts and feelings, there's lots of room for complications and misunderstanding. If we stick to behaviour, things are clearer because behaviour can be observed and measured. As you can see from the chart, writing a report, selling a shirt, coming to work on time, missing a deadline, typing a letter, making a mistake and filling an order are all behaviours.'

'From that list, it seems that behaviour can be either desirable or undesirable', commented the veteran manager.

'Right', said Connelly. 'And how easily you are able to distinguish between the two depends on the goal setting process. You see, if One Minute Goal Setting is done properly, the desired performance is stated in behavioural terms – that is, it can be seen (observed) and counted (measured). That is important because when you observe someone's behaviour you want to be able to determine whether it is contributing towards the accomplishment of the goal (they are doing things right), or taking away from goal achievement (they are doing things wrong). That gives you an idea of how to respond as that person's boss.'

'Respond?' said the veteran manager.

'Responding has to do with consequences', said Connelly. 'The *C* in our ABC's. They are the responses managers give to people when they either perform a task or attempt to perform a task. Consequences follow or come after some performance.'

'One Minute Praisings and One Minute Reprimands are obviously consequences', said the veteran manager.

'A One Minute Praising is an example of a positive consequence or response', said Connelly, 'while a One Minute Reprimand is an example of a negative response. Whether positive or negative, the consequence has to be appropriate.'

'Appropriate?' wondered the veteran manager.

'If you want people to stop doing something, give them a negative response like a One Minute Reprimand', said Connelly. 'But if you want people to keep doing something, or to improve or learn something new, give them a positive consequence like a One Minute Praising.'

'I find that using praisings and reprimands appropriately is not always easy', said the veteran manager.

'It certainly isn't', said Connelly. 'One of the problems is that many managers seem to praise or reprimand their staff depending on how they themselves feel on any given day, regardless of anyone's performance. If they are feeling good, they pat everyone on the back, and if they are in a bad mood, they yell at everyone.'

'And I would imagine that if managers start doing that – praising and reprimanding indiscriminately – their credibility will soon be questioned', said the veteran manager.

'Good point', commented Connelly. 'It reminds me of the story about the blind man who is walking down the street with his guide dog. They get to a corner and while they are waiting for the lights to change, the dog lifts his leg and pees on the blind man's trouser leg. When that happens, the blind man reaches into his pocket and takes out a dog treat. Then he bends down and looks as if he is about to give it to the dog. A bystander who has seen this whole thing can't contain himself any longer so he goes up to the blind man and says, "Sir, it's probably none of my business but I noticed that your dog took a leak on you and now you are about to give him a treat. Do you think that is really a good idea?" The blind man smiles and says, "I'm not about to give my dog a treat. I just want to find out where his head is so I can kick him in the tail."'

'That's beautiful', laughed the veteran. 'When people see a manager isn't credible, that is confusing to them. If the blind man gave the dog a treat for inappropriate behaviour like that and yelled at him when he really wasn't doing anything wrong, the dog would soon become confused and not know what to do. I have seen confusion like that in organisations. Therefore I'd better make sure I understand about consequences.'

'Good idea', said Connelly.

'As I told the One Minute Manager', continued the veteran manager, 'my problem is more confusion about when to be reprimanding and when to be goal setting than any difficulty between reprimanding and praising. Do you have any suggestions?'

'Yes', said Connelly. 'Remember you can effectively reprimand only those who are winners because you can end your negative feedback with a praising like: "You're one of my best people – this recent performance is so unlike you". You can't do that with people who are learning to perform and therefore have no past good performance history.'

'So what do you do when people who are learning make a mistake?' queried the veteran.

'I would go back to goal setting and start again. You can summarise it this way', said Connelly, writing on his pad of paper:

When To Reset Goals And When To Reprimand

If a person:

CAN'T DO *something* → *Go Back to Goal Setting*
(*A Training Problem*)

If a person:

WON'T DO *something* → *Reprimand*
(*An Attitude Problem*)

'That's very helpful', said the veteran. 'So you never reprimand learners.'

'No', said Connelly, 'or you will immobilise them and make them even more insecure'.

'So reprimands do not teach skills', observed the veteran manager. 'They can just change attitudes – get skilled people back to using their abilities.'

'Precisely', said Connelly. 'After you reset goals with someone you are training, you don't leave that person alone. Observe the performance again and then either praise progress or go back to goal setting once more.'

'It seems to me from what you're saying', commented the veteran, 'that there are five steps to training a learner to be a good performer:

1) Tell *what* to do
2) Show *how* to do
3) Let person try
4) Observe performance
5) Praise progress or Redirect

'You've got it in one', said Connelly. 'That's a good summary of how to train someone.'

'What if you keep redirecting some of your staff again and again and they just don't show any progress?' questioned the veteran manager.

'You talk to such a person about career planning', laughed Connelly. 'In other words, he or she just might not be in the right job.'

'Given the importance of redirecting in training', said the veteran, 'why don't you list it as a consequence on your ABC chart?'

'That's a good question', said Connelly. 'Redirect certainly does follow behaviour. But I never thought of it as a consequence. I'll have to add it.'

'I see from the chart, though', said the veteran, 'that you have no response listed as a consequence'.

'It's the most popular with managers', said Connelly. 'So often managers simply ignore their staff's performance, and it doesn't work.'

'What do you mean?' said the veteran manager.

'What happens if you get no response from performing a task?' asked Connelly. 'If your manager doesn't do or say anything?'

'In the beginning, I'd try harder', said the veteran. 'I'd think, "If only I try harder maybe my boss will notice".'

'What if your boss still didn't notice or respond?' asked Connelly.

'After a while, I'd start doing it "half-fast"', smiled the veteran, getting into the pun game that the One Minute Manager and his staff seemed to enjoy. 'Since no one seems to care whether I do this or not, why kill myself.'

'Unless you were doing something that was motivating to you in and of itself', said Connelly.

'If that occurred you would be confused about the difference between work and play', said the veteran manager.

'That's an interesting way to put it', said Connelly. 'If you are doing what you enjoy at work, you will continue to do it well regardless of whether anyone notices and pats you on the back. But generally, no response to good performance, like a negative consequence, tends to decrease the possibility of that performance being repeated.'

'Let me see if I have this straight', said the veteran manager as he showed Connelly his notes:

*

*Only
Positive
Consequences
Encourage
Good
Future
Performance*

*

'That's about it', said Connelly, 'and yet, how do managers most frequently respond to their staff's performance?'

'Negative or no response at all', said the veteran manager. 'As we both know, the attitude of most managers seems to be: when people perform well, do nothing. When people make a mistake, complain.'

'It's the old "leave alone–rebuke" technique', said Connelly. 'Not a very effective way of motivating people.'

'But a very easy habit to fall into', said the veteran manager. 'I've done it myself. I can see now that if I'm going to manage my staff, I'd better learn to manage consequences.'

'That's an important lesson to learn', said Connelly. 'Most people think that activators have a greater influence on performance than consequences. And yet, only 15 to 25 per cent of what affects performance comes from activators like goal setting, while 75 to 85 per cent comes from consequences like praisings and reprimands.'

'You're saying that what happens after a person does something has more impact than what happens before?' questioned the veteran sceptically.

'That's it', said Connelly. 'Performance is determined mainly by consequences. That's why the One Minute Manager is so vehement about the importance of follow-up. We believe you should spend ten times as much time following up your management training as it took to plan and conduct an initial programme. Otherwise people will revert back to old behaviour in a short period of time.'

'Yes, but if you don't set goals, it's unlikely that people will do what you want them to do in the first place', interjected the veteran manager.

'Right', said Connelly. 'But goal setting without any managing of consequences – praising good performance and reprimanding poor – will only get things started and short term success for a manager. In other words, managers will get the performance they want only when they are there, but when they are not there, people may or may not engage in the desired behaviour. We have a saying that emphasises the importance of managing consequences', said Connelly, pointing to a wall plaque.

*

***As A Manager
The Important Thing
Is Not What
Happens When You Are There
But
What Happens When
You Are Not There***

*

'That's so true', said the veteran. 'I can always get the performance I want from people, even from my kids at home, when I am there. But I'm not around all the time. In fact, I think I spend as much, if not more, time at work with my fellow managers at the same level in the organisation and with my boss as I do with my subordinates.'

'So the way you can really tell how good a manager you are', said Connelly, 'is not by what happens when you are there, but by what happens when you're not there. And the secret to getting good performance from your staff when you're not there is how effectively you deliver consequences when you are there – both praisings and reprimands.'

'It is clear to me now', said the veteran manager, 'what you meant when you said activators are important for starting good performance – getting it done the first time – but what really determines and influences whether that desired performance will be repeated when you are not there is what happens after the original performance. The "leave alone–rebuke" approach just frustrates and alienates people.'

'The whole purpose of teaching our people their ABC's', said Connelly, 'is to ensure that they sequence One Minute Goal Setting, One Minute Praisings, and One Minute Reprimands in the proper order. It's a behavioural reminder.'

'You certainly showed me how to begin to turn the secrets into skills', said the veteran. 'I don't think I'll ever forget when to do what any more. But let me ask one more question. You have been emphasising the importance of clear, good goal setting, followed by One Minute Praisings for good performance. I seem to have lost the idea of the effective use of One Minute Reprimands. All we have been talking about is the misuse of reprimands. Could you share with me some of the positive use of reprimands again?'

'You might want to talk to the One Minute Manager about the effective use of One Minute Reprimands', said Connelly. 'He loves to teach that secret, and besides, he would be willing to answer any questions you have about One Minute Goal Setting and One Minute Praisings as well.'

'That's a good idea', said the veteran manager. 'I certainly have taken up enough of your time.'

'That's OK', said Connelly. 'I have enjoyed it. Besides, knowing my ABC's has really helped to give me more free time.'

'I hope it does the same for me', said the veteran.

As the veteran manager left Connelly's office, he found his mind going a mile a minute. Connelly had been quite helpful. As he approached the One Minute Manager's office, the manager's secretary smiled. 'Did you have a good meeting with Tom Connelly?' she asked.

'I certainly did', the veteran manager replied, returning her smile. 'Could I see the boss?'

'Go straight in', she said. 'He was wondering if you were coming back.'

As the veteran entered the office, he found the One Minute Manager looking out of his favourite window. He turned as he heard the veteran manager enter.

'You were with Connelly for quite a while. The two of you must have got along quite well', he said.

'It was most helpful', said the veteran. 'But I have some concerns about the use of reprimands', he went on. 'In teaching me the ABC's, Connelly seemed to stress the importance of praisings but played down the use of reprimands. I know you believe in delivering bad news sometimes. Maybe I just need some reorientation.'

'The best way for me to respond to your concerns about reprimanding', replied the One Minute Manager, 'is to start by talking about managing winners – people with proven track records. Winners are easy to supervise. All you have to do is set up One Minute goals and then they are off.'

'It's the same in my experience', said the veteran manager. 'While everyone likes a pat on the back once in a while, you don't have to praise winners very much. They usually beat you to the punch. Apart from not praising winners very much, you don't often have to reprimand them either, do you?'

'No!' said the One Minute Manager. 'Good performers are usually self-correcting. If they make a mistake, they fix it before anyone else notices.'

'But everyone makes mistakes sometimes that they are unaware of', stated the veteran manager.

'In that case, you may have to reprimand', said the One Minute Manager. 'However, good performers don't resent it because of the way you deliver that reprimand if they know the three secrets.'

'I assume you are talking about ending the reprimand with a praising', wondered the veteran manager.

'Precisely', said the One Minute Manager.

'Connelly cleared up for me why you don't reprimand a learner, but I still have trouble understanding why you praise someone at the end of a reprimand', said the veteran manager.

'Remember, you reprimand only when you know the person can do better', the One Minute Manager reminded him. 'When you leave your staff after a reprimand, you want them to be thinking about what they did wrong, not about the way you treated them.'

'I don't understand', the veteran hesitated.

'Let me see if I can explain it this way', said the One Minute Manager. 'Most people not only don't end their reprimands with a praising, but they also give the person a parting shot: "If you think you're going to get promoted, you have another think coming". Now when you leave that person, especially if there is a co-worker within earshot, what do you think they will be talking about? How you treated the person you were reprimanding, or what the person did wrong?'

'How you treated the person', said the veteran manager.

'Precisely', said the One Minute Manager. 'They're talking about how awful you are. And yet that person did something wrong. If you end your reprimand with a praising, you will be telling the person, "You are OK but your behaviour isn't!" Then when you leave, the person will be thinking about what he or she did wrong. If for any reason he tries to complain about you to co-workers, they will stop it by saying, "What are you getting so excited about? He said you were one of his best people. He just doesn't want you to make that mistake again."'

'I think I understand what you're saying about ending with a praising', said the veteran manager. 'See if this is a good summary comment', as he showed his notes to the One Minute Manager. They said:

*

*When You
End A Reprimand
With A Praising
People Think
About* Their *Behaviour
Not
Your Behaviour*

*

Effective Reprimanding / 41

As the One Minute Manager read what the veteran had written, he smiled and said, 'That's very well put. Let me give you a personal example to illustrate the importance of what you are saying. One Friday night, shortly after I had learned about the One Minute Reprimand, my wife came into the room where I was reading the evening paper. I always know that there is something wrong and I am about to get the problem dumped in my lap when she says, "Great manager of people . . ." That's exactly what she said that night. Then she continued, "I just caught Karen (our 15-year-old daughter) sneaking out of the house with a bottle of vodka on the way to a party. She said it wasn't for her; it was for her older friends."

'"The drivers!" I guessed.

'"I think I'll kill her", said my wife. "Could you take over?"

'My wife and I always had a strategy: if one of us felt out of control of a situation, we threw the ball to the other. I have a lot of sympathy for single parents who have no one to turn to in such situations.

'Since I had just learned about the reprimand, I thought this might be a good opportunity to see if it worked. I said, "Where is Karen?" My wife told me she was in the kitchen. So I went straight out to the kitchen and found Karen standing there looking as though she were about to be sent to prison. I walked up to her and put my hand gently on her shoulder. I said, "Karen, Mum tells me she just caught you sneaking out of the house with a bottle of vodka. Let me tell you how I feel about that. I can't believe it. How many times have I told you the way kids get killed is to have some kid drinking and driving. And to be sneaking around with a bottle of vodka . . ."

'Now I knew that the rule of the reprimand was that you have only about thirty seconds to share your feelings.'

'I bet you wanted two hours', said the veteran manager.

'How right you are', laughed the One Minute Manager. 'Some parents take a whole weekend. You catch one of your kids doing something wrong on Friday night and you give the kid a row. Half an hour later you see the same kid and you say, "Let me tell you one other thing..." Then you see the kid the next morning and you say, "Let me tell you about your friends too..." You spend the whole weekend making yourself and the kid miserable over one misbehaviour.

'The rule about the reprimand is that you have only thirty seconds to share your feelings about what the person did wrong, and when it's over – it's over. Don't keep nagging the person for the same mistake.

'Recognising all this, I had to come to a screeching halt in sharing my feelings with Karen. It was at this point that I realised the importance of pausing for a moment of silence between sharing your feelings and the last part of the reprimand. It permits you to calm down and at the same time lets the person you are reprimanding feel the intensity of your feelings. So I took a deep breath while Karen was swallowing hard. Then I said, "Let me tell you one other thing, Karen. I love you. You're a really responsible kid. Mum and I normally don't have to worry about you. It sounds like some other kid. You're better than that. That's why Mum and I are not going to let you get away with that kind of thing."

'Then I gave her a hug and said, "Now get off to the party, but remember: you're better than that".'

'I'm not sure I would have let her go to the party after something like that', said the veteran. 'I bet she couldn't believe it herself.'

'She couldn't believe it', confirmed the One Minute Manager. 'But I told her, "Now you know how I feel about teenage drinking and sneaking around. I know you're not going to do that again, so have a good time."

'In the past, before I knew about the One Minute Reprimand, not only would I not have ended her reprimand with a praising, I would have sent her to her room, screaming something like "You're not going to another party until you're twenty-five".

'Now, if I had sent her to her room, what do you think she would have been thinking about? What she did wrong or how I had treated her?' said the One Minute Manager.

'How you had treated her', said the veteran manager. 'I bet she would have been on the phone immediately, telling her friends what a monster you were. Teenagers love to share parent stories.'

'Absolutely', said the One Minute Manager. 'And then she would have been psychologically off the hook for what she had done wrong, with all her attention focused on how I had treated her.'

'What happened next?' asked the veteran, feeling he was in the middle of a soap opera.

'The next morning', continued the One Minute Manager, 'when I was eating breakfast, Karen came downstairs. Wondering how I had done, I said to her, "Karen, how did you like the way I dealt with the vodka incident last night?"

'"I hated it", she said. "You ruined the party for me."

'"I ruined the party for you?"

'"Yes", she said. "Because all through the evening I kept thinking about what I had done and how much I had disappointed you and Mum!"

'I smiled to myself and thought, "It worked! It really worked! She was concentrating on what she had done wrong and not on how I had treated her."'

'That was a very helpful, clear example', said the veteran manager. 'I think I've got that part of the reprimand, but I'd like to ask you a couple of other things about the One Minute Reprimand.'

'Fire away', said the One Minute Manager. 'Most of the questions we get about One Minute Management have to do with the reprimand.'

'What if the person you are reprimanding – Karen, for example – starts to argue with you?' said the veteran.

'You stop what you are saying right away', said the One Minute Manager, 'and make it very clear to that person that this is not a discussion. "I am sharing my feelings about what you did wrong, and if you want to discuss it later, I will. But right now this is not a two-way discussion. I am telling you how I feel."'

'That's helpful', said the veteran. 'One other thing. If I accept the principle of praising someone at the end of a reprimand, why not begin a reprimand with a praising? When I did reprimands in the past, I used the "sandwich approach": pat them on the back, kick them, pat them on the back.'

'I know that style well', said the One Minute Manager, 'but I've learned that it is very important to keep praisings and reprimands separate. If you start a reprimand with a praising, then you will ruin the impact of your praising.'

'Why?' asked the veteran manager.

'Because when you go to see a person just to praise him', said the One Minute Manager, 'he will not hear your praising because he will be wondering when the other shoe will drop – what bad news will follow the good'.

'So by keeping praisings and reprimands in order, you will let your staff hear both more clearly', summarised the veteran. 'What about more tangible punishments like demotion, being transferred, or some other penalty? Are they ever appropriate?'

'Our experience with the One Minute Reprimand', said the One Minute Manager, 'suggests that you do not usually need to add some additional penalty. It is an uncomfortable enough experience.'

'That was beautifully illustrated with Karen', said the veteran manager. 'I think you really cleared up my questions about reprimands. And also now, I can see how learning the ABC's helps managers take their knowledge of One Minute Management and translate it into action. But how can you integrate One Minute Management into a total organisational programme for performance improvement?'

'You have to pay the PRICE', said the One Minute Manager with a smile.

'What is that?' asked the veteran manager.

'The PRICE system', said the One Minute Manager, 'goes beyond the ABC's by providing managers with five easy-to-follow steps that can involve everyone in improving performance'.

'It sounds fascinating', said the veteran, 'but my head is already swimming from all that I have learned today'.

'Why don't you stay overnight locally and we can get together at nine in the morning? I'll ask my secretary to make a reservation for you at the Osborn Hotel. The manager there is really excited about One Minute Management and has implemented a unique praising programme designed to catch his employees doing things right. I think you will find it most interesting.'

'Sounds good to me', said the veteran.

WHEN the veteran manager arrived at the hotel, he went straight to the registration desk. As he was checking in, the receptionist said to the veteran, 'Our customers are important to us. I wonder if I can ask you to do us a favour during your visit?'

'Of course', said the veteran, surprised by this request. 'What is it?'

'We'd like you to take this book of "praising coupons". If any of our employees treats you or another guest the way you like to be treated, would you tear off a coupon, write on the back what the employee did right, find out what his or her name is, and hand it in at the manager's office.'

'So all your customers are catching your employees doing things right', laughed the veteran. 'I bet a praising comes with each coupon the manager receives.'

'You read *The One Minute Manager*', exclaimed the receptionist with a smile.

'I did. Your hotel really seems to be putting One Minute Management to work', said the veteran.

'It's a fantastic system!' responded the receptionist enthusiastically. 'Have a nice evening.'

After an early dinner, the veteran went straight to his room to relax. He was amazed by how well he had been treated by all the hotel employees. He had already filled in three coupons - for the porter, his waitress, and the maitre d'hotel. Catching people doing things right was changing his whole attitude towards this hotel. The praising coupons made it his job as a guest not to complain but to compliment.

The next morning, the veteran manager packed his bags and headed downstairs. After having breakfast he checked out. On his way out of the hotel, he called in at the manager's office to drop off his praising coupons. The manager happened to be there.

As he handed the manager his praising coupons, the veteran manager said, 'I think this praising programme of yours is a great idea. It's a very practical way to put One Minute Management to work. Have there been any tangible bottom line effects of the programme?'

'Although we have had the system in operation for only five months or so', said the hotel manager, 'we have already seen significant reductions in absenteeism and staff turnover. Our employees look forward to coming to work now because they are anxious to see if they can be caught doing something right. And we have not been giving any financial payoffs for coupons - just a pat on the back for a job well done.'

'Do you think this programme has changed the customers' attitudes, too?' wondered the veteran.

'Absolutely!' said the hotel manager. 'Our greatest improvement has been in guest inspection scores. Our guests are asked to rate the hotel on an ABCDE scale on such items as value/cost, appearance, service, and friendliness. Prior to the praising programme, less than 70 per cent of the guests who filled out the guest inspection cards rated the hotel in the A to B range. After the first five months of the programme the scores are averaging over 90 per cent A's and B's and we are getting three times as many returned cards.'

'So your praising coupons are paying high dividends for you, your customers, and your employees', said the veteran manager.

'Yes', said the hotel manager. 'Putting the One Minute Manager to work pays a good return on investment.'

As the veteran manager shook hands with the hotel manager, he smiled and said, 'My stay here has been very profitable for me too!'

WHEN the veteran arrived at the One Minute Manager's office, he found him in his usual pose by the window. When he sensed the veteran standing in the doorway, the One Minute Manager turned round and greeted him with a friendly handshake and offered the veteran a chair at the conference table.

'Well, did you enjoy your stay at the Osborn Hotel last night?' the One Minute Manager asked as he sat down.

'I certainly did', responded the veteran, 'and you were right – it was unique!'

'I wanted you to experience', confided the One Minute Manager, 'an attempt to put One Minute Management to work before we talked today. I thought it would help you understand our PRICE system better.'

As the veteran manager was listening to the One Minute Manager, he noticed a new plaque on his desk. It read:

*

*Don't Just Do Something –
Sit There*

*

The veteran manager smiled because he knew how the usual frantic, yet inefficient, pace of most organisations demanded the opposite.

'My key people gave it to me', said the One Minute Manager, when he saw the veteran looking at the plaque. 'They thought it symbolised the importance of goal setting as a means of avoiding the "activity trap".'

'The activity trap?' wondered the veteran manager.

'That's where people are running around trying to do things right before anyone has stopped to work out what are the right things to do.'

'Talking about doing things right', said the veteran, 'what's the best way for me to learn PRICE?'

'Why don't you go and talk to Alice Smith', suggested the One Minute Manager. 'She's one of our most creative managers. She helped us develop the PRICE system. Since she took over our sales operation, sales have skyrocketed.'

As the One Minute Manager was ringing Alice Smith, the veteran manager was smiling to himself. He thought, 'They certainly have taken all the mystique out of managing people. I'll bet PRICE is really quite simple, but powerful.'

'Well, Alice is all set to see you', said the One Minute Manager. 'You can go over to her office straight away. She is in the same building as Connelly but on the third floor.'

WHEN the veteran manager got to Alice Smith's office, he found her working quietly at her desk. He thought to himself, 'At last a One Minute Manager who seems to be doing some work'.

She smiled as he entered. 'So you want to know if the PRICE is right', she said as she beckoned the veteran to sit down.

'Corny but true', said the veteran. 'I'm anxious to get started.'

'That's important because the PRICE system is the nuts and bolts of how to put the One Minute Manager to work and make a difference every day with the performance and satisfaction of people on the job. But you have to listen carefully because now we take the basic three skills and turn them into five important steps.'

Smith immediately went to the small blackboard behind her desk and wrote:

> Pinpoint
> Record
> Involve
> Coach
> Evaluate

'*Pinpoint* is a process of defining key performance areas for people in observable measurable terms', started Smith. 'In essence, it is the performance areas that you would identify as One Minute Goals.'

'Suppose I told you I had a morale problem in my work group', said the veteran manager, 'and I wanted to rekindle commitment from my staff. Would that be specific enough?'

'No', said Smith. 'We can't do anything about morale problems, poor attitudes, laziness, or things like that.'

'Isn't it important to deal with morale problems in organisations?' asked the veteran manager.

'Of course it is, but I would have to pinpoint what you mean by poor morale', explained Smith. 'Do you mean people are coming to work late, or quality rejects are frequent, or people are bickering at work? What do you mean by poor morale?'

'So we need to stop managers from saying things are good or bad', said the veteran, 'and get them to identify specifically what is happening'.

'That's what pinpointing is all about', said Smith, pleased by the veteran's ability to learn quickly. 'Establishing the areas you are going to measure and how you are going to measure them – for example, quantity, quality, cost (on or off budget), or timeliness.'

'Where does that bring us?' interrupted the veteran.

'Direct to *Record*', answered Smith. 'Once you have pinpointed a performance problem or One Minute Goal, you want to be able to measure present performance and keep track of progress in that area.'

'You mean you would gather actual data on how often people are late to work, how frequently products are rejected because of quality, and the like?' said the veteran.

'That's right', said Smith. 'You want to take the guesswork out of performance improvement.'

'What if someone says "You can't measure performance in my job!"' wondered the veteran manager.

'When people tell us that', said Smith, 'we suggest that maybe we should eliminate their position and see if we've lost anything. It's amazing how interested they suddenly get in establishing ways to identify goals and measure performance in their job.'

'Could you give me an example', said the veteran, 'of a performance problem you eliminated through the PRICE system?'

'Yes', said Smith. 'When I took over the department, the old sales manager told me, "The problem here is phone contact. Salespeople never make appointments with customers by phone. They think they have to be on the road all the time. When they get to the customer, he's often out for the morning, or he's busy and can't be interrupted. They have to wait to see him so they end up spending all their time in coffee shops. If they made appointments, they'd get twice as much done in half the time."

'I asked, "How do you know phone contact is a problem?"

'"I just feel all the problems start there", he replied. "That's always been a problem in this company."

'Then I asked, "Have you counted it? Is there any way to tell exactly the number of phone calls salespeople make to customers?"

'"Well", he said, "I could check their phone logs. Each salesperson is required to keep a daily log of calls beside his or her phone."

'When I checked it, I found that making appointments was not a crucial issue for everyone. In fact, only three salespeople were delinquent in their phoning', Smith stated.

'By recording or measuring performance', said the veteran, 'you attempt to make sure the problem is real and not just a feeling. You don't want to fix what isn't broken.'

'Precisely', said Smith. 'It's most effective to plot the information on a graph', she explained as she pulled a folder from her desk file. 'Here's an initial graph I made of appointment calls for one of my problem salespeople, Jack.

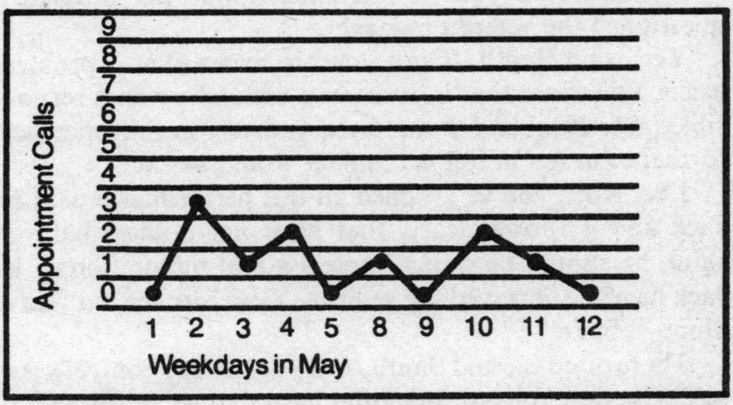

'On any of the graphs we use, we put time across the bottom or horizontal axis, and the pinpointed behaviour along the side or the vertical axis', explained Smith. 'The time element for Jack was weekdays in May for a two-week period and the behaviour was the number of appointment calls made each day.'

'After I made the graph I calculated Jack's mean number of daily appointment calls. Over two weeks, he averaged one call a day. I knew we had a problem and that there was a difference between actual performance and what I thought was desired performance. I was ready for the *Involve* step in PRICE.'

'Is that when you inform Jack about the problem?' questioned the veteran manager.

'Yes', said Smith. 'Once you are aware that a problem exists, you share that information with whoever is responsible (accountable) for that area and/or can influence performance in it – in our example it would be Jack.'

'I bet when you've graphed all this performance data on Jack and it shows clearly that he is not doing what you think he should be doing, there's a real temptation to let Jack have it', observed the veteran. 'Give him the old "leave alone–rebuke".'

'There often is', said Smith, 'but you need to control yourself. The time for reprimanding hasn't come yet. In fact, it is important to remember that graphs are not meant to be used as weapons, or as evidence in a managerial prosecution. They are designed to be used as training tools as well as non-judgmental methods of feedback.'

'So how do you share your graph with Jack?' asked the veteran.

'Without judgment', said Smith, 'and in a spirit of learning. You want Jack to learn, and you assume that Jack wants to improve. You know the saying here:

*

*Feedback
Is The
Breakfast
Of
Champions*

*

'How true that is', affirmed the veteran. 'But tell me, how do you involve someone like Jack besides giving him feedback on results?'

'You involve him in establishing the activators', said Smith. 'That is, deciding what has to be agreed upon before Jack can be expected to improve his performance to the desired level.'

'Besides goal setting, what other agreements do you have to set up?' smiled the veteran, enjoying the opportunity to show off what he had already learned.

'Coaching and evaluation strategies', answered Smith. 'You need to agree about how you are going to supervise Jack as well as how he will be evaluated and what pay-off he can anticipate for improved performance.'

'Do you always involve your people in establishing One Minute Goals?' wondered the veteran manager.

'Yes', said Smith. *One Minute Management just doesn't work unless you share it with your staff.* Otherwise they will think you are trying to manipulate them. That is particularly true with goal setting. Shared goal setting tends to get greater commitment from people and guarantees the setting of a realistic goal for the performance area.'

'A realistic goal?' puzzled the veteran manager.

'A realistic goal is moderately difficult but achievable', explained Smith. 'It's acceptable to you as a manager and it's possible for your members of staff to accomplish. Let's go back to Jack. He has been setting up one appointment a day by phone. How many appointment calls are acceptable to you? How many are attainable by Jack?'

'How many does the best salesperson make?' inquired the veteran manager.

'Comparing Jack to the best won't encourage him. It will only discourage him', answered Smith. 'Remember we're using this method as a training tool, not as a punishment.'

'What goal would you set?' asked the veteran, shrugging his shoulders.

'I'd probably say, "Jack, let's see if you can make three appointment calls a day next week. How does that sound?"'

'So you have to be specific about the number and the time span', commented the veteran.

'Exactly', said Smith. 'What do you suppose would happen if I simply said to Jack, "I'd like you to make more appointment calls. I don't think you have been making enough lately."?'

'He'd probably say OK', said the veteran, 'and then not take it seriously'.

'That's why I'd make a graph with Jack by my side', said Smith. 'Then he'd know I was serious and know exactly what he had to do to get back into my good books.'

62 / Involve People

She removed another graph from the file she had taken from her desk. 'This was Jack's first goal setting graph', said Smith as she handed the veteran the graph.

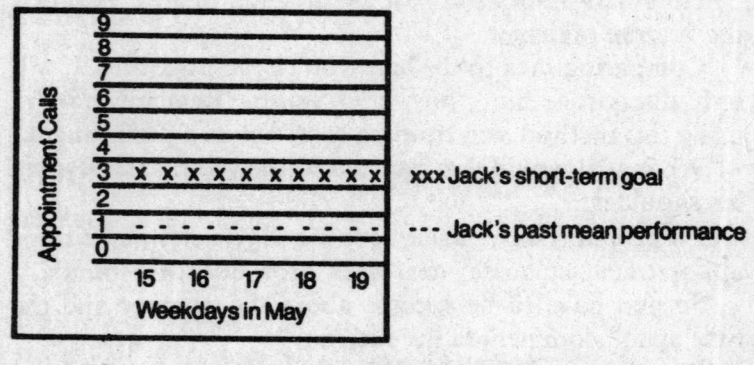

```
Appointment Calls
9
8
7
6
5
4
3   x x x x x x x x x x    xxx Jack's short-term goal
2
1   - - - - - - - - - -    --- Jack's past mean performance
0
    15  16  17  18  19
    Weekdays in May
```

'You see, we plotted Jack's past mean performance (one call a day) and his short-term goal (three calls a day). That way he could see the difference between what he'd been doing and where he was going', explained Smith.

'Why wouldn't you say you wanted Jack to make an appointment call for every sales visit he was going to make?' wondered the veteran.

'That might have been an appropriate goal in the long-term', said Smith, 'but in the short-term you couldn't expect that kind of turnaround in behaviour because Jack had obviously got himself into some bad work patterns. In the same way, you can't expect to lose twenty-five pounds in weight in one day, but you do want some change. So we had to set a short-term goal with Jack, like three appointment calls a day.'

'Short-term goal?' wondered the veteran.

'It's a first step', said Smith. 'When you set up a performance-improvement programme with someone, remember not to set the end-result goal (in this case an appointment call for *every* sales visit – about six or seven calls per workday) as the goal that has to be reached before someone can feel a sense of accomplishment and deserve a praising; otherwise you might have to wait forever.'

'I remember that concept now', said the veteran. 'In the beginning, when working on performance, you need to set things up so you can catch people doing things approximately right (short-term goal), not exactly right (final goal).'

'Precisely', said Smith. 'The journey to exactly right is made up of a whole series of approximately rights.'

'So you are saying, "Rome wasn't built in a day"', said the veteran. 'As a result, what you want to do is keep track of progress from the present level of performance to the desired level. What's the best way to do that?'

'By involving people in coaching', said Smith. 'As you know, once people have a clear idea about what they are being asked to do, coaching is essentially observing their performance and giving them feedback on results. But the whole coaching process is set up by agreeing in advance with your staff when and how you are going to give them feedback. That part of coaching is done during the *Involve* step.'

'I would imagine', interrupted the veteran, 'that by designing, together with your staff, the feedback system you are going to use, you are increasing the chances of their winning – accomplishing their goals'.

'Exactly', said Smith. 'Setting up a good feedback system through performance graphs is crucial if you hope to do any day-to-day coaching. That's why, with Jack, we agreed that for the first week I'd go and see him at his desk every day and review his phone log. I'd graph his performance and share it with him.'

'What other agreements about coaching did you make with him besides your daily visits?' wondered the veteran manager.

'Recording performance every day can be time-consuming', said Smith. 'So we agreed to meet again after the first week to evaluate when Jack could begin to administer his own feedback.'

'Administer his own feedback?' repeated the veteran.

'If I am having a performance problem with Jack, what I want to do is set up a graph that Jack is able to use. He can put his own check marks, stars, or whatever, on the graph.'

'Then he's able to say, "Hey, I'm doing better", or "I'm doing worse"', suggested the veteran manager. 'He can even begin to praise or reprimand himself.'

'Yes', said Smith. 'Feedback that is self-administered can be immediate – as close to the performance as possible.'

'At this point, what else did you involve Jack in?' said the veteran.

'All I had left to do in the *I* step in the PRICE system was to involve Jack in performance evaluation', said Smith.

'How did you intend to do that?' asked the veteran manager.

'When we set up the graph, Jack knew how his performance was going to be evaluated, but to complete his involvement in performance evaluation, we still had to decide what was in it for Jack if he improved', said Smith.

'What do you mean?' asked the veteran.

'What positive consequence will happen for Jack if he reaches his goal', Smith answered.

'Did I hear you say that you and Jack had to decide together? Don't you just tell him?' responded the veteran.

'If Jack had been less capable and committed, I would have determined the rewards, but Jack was a very creative man. He knew best what rewards would motivate him', explained Smith. 'I asked Jack, "What will motivate you to make more calls?" He said, "If I make my quota, write me a note. I collect those things. I have every letter of commendation I've received since school. But don't get your secretary to type me some form letter. You write it by hand."

'I thought that was a great idea. I said, "What if you don't meet your quota?" He said, "Come and tell me I deserve a reprimand. You probably won't even have to deliver it. But just knowing that you know I am slipping back to old behaviour will get me back on track."'

'Did you keep track of the number of praisings versus the number of reprimands?' laughed the veteran.

'It might sound funny', said Smith, 'but I did exactly that. I started a log of praisings and reprimands. It worked beautifully. Now I keep a praising/reprimand log on all my employees. It's just a list of names with P's and R's after each name with a shorthand note about what happened. It helps me keep track of One Minute Management.'

'That makes sense', said the veteran manager. 'So prior to actually coaching or evaluating performance, the consequences for goal accomplishment have to be agreed upon in the Involve (I) step of the PRICE system.'

'In Jack's case', said Smith, 'he knew what the goals (short- and long-term) were, how I was going to supervise or coach him, and how his performance would be evaluated, including the consequences he could expect for poor performance as well as for improved performance'.

'Now that all those things were settled', interrupted the veteran, 'Jack was ready to start improving his appointment-call behaviour'.

'Yes', said Smith. 'And at that point, my role changed from involving Jack in decision-making about establishing the necessary activators to observing his performance and managing the consequences.'

'That's what coaching is all about', said the veteran. 'Observing behaviour and giving feedback on results – both praisings and reprimands. And that's when you began the *C* or *Coach* step in PRICE.'

'You've got it. Now I can show you how well Jack did', said Smith. 'Here's his graph from the first week.'

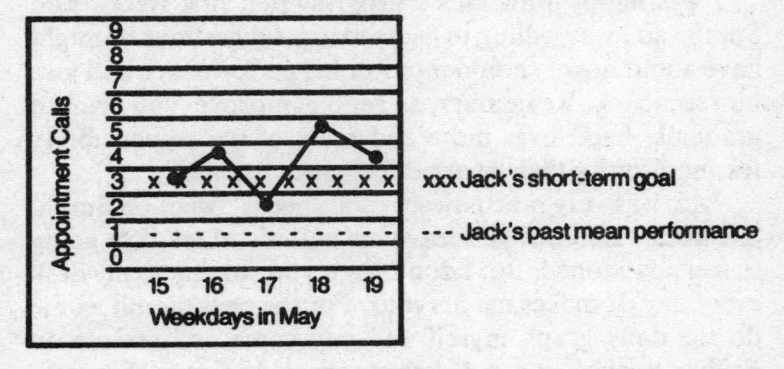

```
Appointment Calls
9
8
7
6
5
4
3  x x x x x x x x x       xxx Jack's short-term goal
2
1  - - - - - - - - - -     --- Jack's past mean performance
0
   15  16  17  18  19
   Weekdays in May
```

'That's great. He bettered his goal except on the third day', commented the veteran manager as he read the graph. 'When did you tell him about his improvement – at your planned meeting at the end of the week?'

'Absolutely not', said Smith. 'Remember a basic rule of feedback is that it should be immediate and specific. If the data flow is vague and delayed, it is not an effective training tool. And besides, I had made an agreement with Jack that during the first week I'd go and see him every day, review his phone log, graph his performance and share it with him.'

'How specific would you be?' wondered the veteran manager.

'I'd actually use numbers', said Smith. 'I'd say, "You made your goal, you bettered your goal by one or you missed your goal by one". So once the goal is set, feedback relates specifically to the goal.'

'OK. I see how the daily feedback with Jack went', said the veteran, 'but how did you handle the meeting at the end of the week when you planned to evaluate whether Jack could begin to administer his own feedback or not?'

'I was happy with Jack's progress that first week', said Smith, 'so I was willing to listen to any suggestions he might have about how I should monitor his performance and give him feedback. Remember, as people improve, you want to gradually hand over more and more of the responsibility for monitoring their own performance to them.

'Jack was very much aware of his needs', went on Smith. 'He said, "Look, if you leave me entirely alone, I'm going to feel abandoned. But I don't want you coming to my desk every day. It makes me nervous. For the next month let me do the daily graph myself and you come and see me on Fridays to check it out. If I need some help during the week, I'll come to see you."'

'So you worked out a new agreement with him', said the veteran. 'Did you keep doing that until he performed like a winner in that part of his job?'

'Absolutely', said Smith. 'I want to supervise my people closely only if they need it. As soon as they can perform on their own, I am ready to let go. In coaching you want to schedule fewer and fewer feedback meetings as people move gradually from their present level of performance to the desired level of performance. We have an expression that we use here, that I think would be important for you to learn.' She wrote on her pad:

*

*Achieving
Good Performance
For
Most People
Is
A Journey –
Not
A Destination*

*

'That's well put', said the veteran. 'Many managers just shout out destinations (goals) and then sit back and wait for people to reach them. What's helpful about the PRICE system is that it suggests that coaching is a process of managing the journey. I'm ready to move on to *Evaluate* (E), the last step in the PRICE system. Are you?'

'Why not?' said Smith. 'After all, evaluation and coaching go hand in hand. In fact, every time you give someone feedback you are evaluating. You want to continually determine how well performance is going in pinpointed areas. Are you getting the results you want? If not, why?'

'If evaluation and coaching go hand in hand', said the veteran manager, 'why do you have *evaluate* as a separate step in the PRICE system?'

'Because most organisations have actual formal performance review sessions', said the veteran. 'These sessions are held quarterly, semi-annually, or only once a year. In the PRICE system we recommend that you graph and track performance in pinpointed One Minute Goal areas for no longer than six weeks without having a formal evaluation session – unless the person is a proven winner.'

'What do you discuss in these sessions?' wondered the veteran.

'Nothing new', said Smith. 'Remember, praisings and reprimands must be delivered as close to the performance as possible. No saving up. All we do is review what we have been talking about throughout the coaching process. The main question at these evaluation sessions is to decide whether you want to keep the performance area as a PRICE project or assume it is now fixed or accomplished and the people involved can give themselves their own feedback. If the performance is still not up to the desired level, then you start the process again.'

'While evaluation in the PRICE system is a continuous process', said the veteran, 'I don't get the feeling it is a punitive process. In putting One Minute Management to work, you are not trying to trip people up.'

'David Berlo, one of the most thoughtful teachers and consultants I have ever met', said Smith, 'gave me the best expression of that philosophy. He got interested in the training of whales. One day he asked some of his training friends whether they actually trained the whales by using some of the concepts we have been talking about in the coaching process. They said, "Yes, with one addition".'

'What was that?' wondered the veteran.

'Before they attempted to train the whales to do anything', said Smith, 'the trainers told David, "We feed them and make sure they're not hungry. And then we jump in the water and play with the whales until we have convinced them . . ."'

'Convinced them of what?' wondered the veteran manager.

'Let me write that down for you', said Smith, 'because it underlies everything that One Minute Management stands for'. She reached over and borrowed the veteran manager's notepad and began to write.

*We
Mean
Them
No
Harm*

'That's a powerful statement', said the veteran manager as he read what Alice Smith had written. 'That's all about trust, isn't it?'

'It certainly is', said Smith. 'David is writing a book entitled *I Mean You No Harm* because he feels that most of the performance review and evaluation systems that companies set up in our country suggest the very opposite.'

'Now that you mention it', said the veteran, 'that is so true. Most evaluation systems suggest that there always have to be winners and losers.'

'That's just not part of the philosophy of the One Minute Manager', said Smith.

'So when you talk about evaluation in the PRICE system', said the veteran, 'you are always trying to find out whether you are getting the desired results. If you are, your staff get recognised and praised. And if you're not, they get redirected or reprimanded depending on whether the problem is one of ability or motivation. Are there any other reasons why you wouldn't be getting the desired results?'

'Performance can break down at every step of the PRICE system', responded Smith. 'You might have pinpointed an irrelevant area. Or you might be recording data ineffectively. In involving your staff you might have agreed upon too low or too high a goal, your feedback might be erratic or your consequences not sufficiently motivating.'

'So you are taking some significant responsibility for ensuring that your staff perform well', said the veteran manager.

'Most definitely', said Smith. 'My job as a manager is not just to sit back, cross my arms, look stern and evaluate. It's to roll up my sleeves and be responsive to people and what they need to perform well.'

'So you have to keep your eyes and ears open', interjected the veteran. 'I would imagine you often go back to Pinpoint, and start the process again. So PRICE is a continuous process.'

'Exactly', said Smith. 'That's why we like to show PRICE almost like a dial on the telephone', she said, pointing to a plaque on the wall. It read:

A Summary of the PRICE SYSTEM

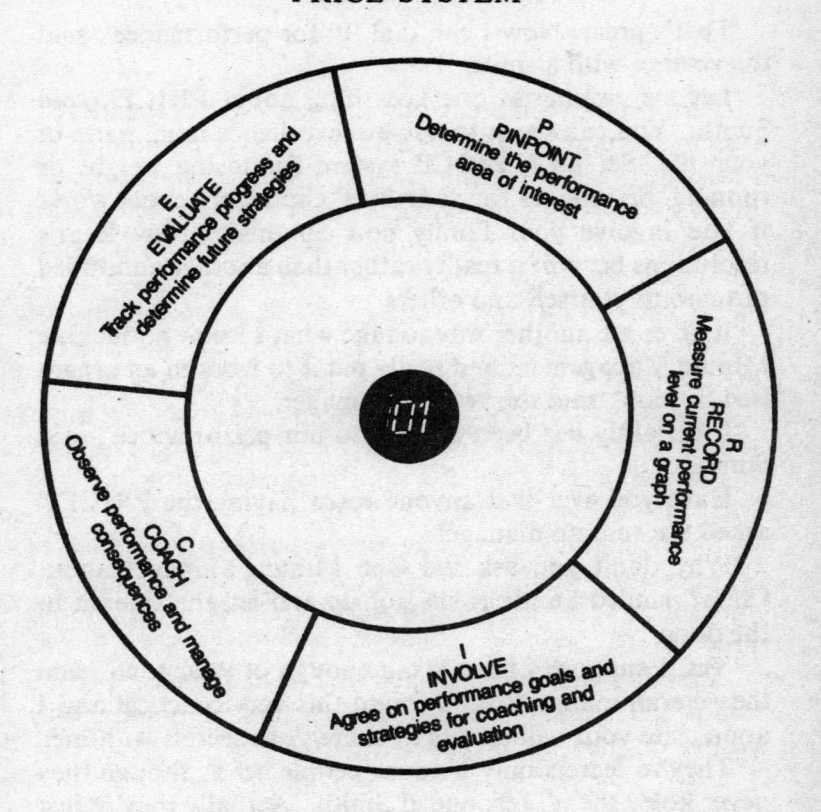

- **P — PINPOINT**: Determine the performance area of interest
- **R — RECORD**: Measure current performance level on a graph
- **I — INVOLVE**: Agree on performance goals and strategies for coaching and evaluation
- **C — COACH**: Observe performance and manage consequences
- **E — EVALUATE**: Track performance progress and determine future strategies

'That's great. Now I can dial 'P' for performance', said the veteran with a smile.

'Let me emphasise one last thing about PRICE', said Smith. 'You can use it to achieve excellence in all parts of your life. Set up a PRICE system for losing weight or running. Set one up for your kids' chores or school work. If you involve your family you can make New Year's resolutions become a reality rather than another unfulfilled promise to yourself and others.'

'It gives me another way to take what I know about One Minute Management and really put it to work in an organised fashion', said the veteran manager.

'It certainly has been the key to our performance', said Smith.

'Have you ever had anyone resist paying the PRICE?' asked the veteran manager.

'Why don't you ask the One Minute Manager about Chris?' smiled Smith as she got up and led the veteran to the door.

'Yes, I suppose I have taken enough of your time', said the veteran manager. 'I've found this very practical and I appreciate your willingness to share your secrets with me.'

'They're secrets only because people act as though they never knew them', responded Smith. 'Actually they're just common sense put to use.'

As the veteran walked back to the One Minute Manager's office, he was amazed at how true that phrase was – common sense put to use.

When he got to the One Minute Manager's office, the veteran was greeted with a warm smile. 'The PRICE is right, isn't it?' the One Minute Manager laughed.

'It certainly is', said the veteran manager. 'It really makes sense, but I have one question. Who is Chris?'

The One Minute Manager began to laugh. 'I thought it was only a matter of time before someone told you about Chris. Why don't you sit down', said the One Minute Manager, 'so I can tell you about Chris'.

'When I first came here I heard about Chris from Steve Mulvany, a productivity-improvement consultant who had worked with our company. Steve said, "Watch out for Chris when you start training the foremen about One Minute Management. He's a real tough guy." I got the impression that converting Chris to One Minute Management would be like persuading a charging rhino to rethink his strategy.

'The stories about Chris were widespread. He was almost a legend in his own time. For instance, I was told that one time he was so enraged by one of his staff in the morning that he literally (I checked it out later with Chris and it was true) picked him up and hung him by his overalls on a nail and left him there until lunch.'

'Now, how could anybody do that?' asked the veteran manager.

'Chris is about five feet nine by five feet nine and strong', said the One Minute Manager. 'When he sits at the end of our thirty-inch-wide conference table he is about as wide as the table. He has arms as big as my thighs. His head sits on his shoulders as if he had no neck.'

'He doesn't sound like a very attractive human being', said the veteran.

'No, he's not – or at least he wasn't', said the One Minute Manager. 'His eyes were bloodshot, he had a grumpy voice, and he walked like a bear on the prowl.

'I first met Chris', continued the One Minute Manager, 'at a training session. When I came here and began to implement One Minute Management, I initially did most of the training myself. I arrived early to the session where I met Chris. While I was setting up training materials in the front of the conference room, I suddenly got the feeling somebody was watching me. I turned round and there was Chris sitting alone at the other end of the conference room.'

'How did you know it was him?' asked the veteran manager.

'I just knew', said the One Minute Manager. 'Especially when I got no response to a smile. I could just feel his eyes looking through me.'

'What did you say?' interrupted the veteran. 'I feel as if I'm in the middle of another soap opera.'

'Nothing then', said the One Minute Manager, 'but I knew he was watching my every move. At least I sensed he was. When I started my session he sat quietly until I said, "One of the keys to motivating your people is to catch them doing something right. When that occurs", I asked, "what should you do as a manager?" Everyone said reward or praise them, except Chris.'

'How did you know he didn't agree?' said the veteran manager.

'Chris raised his hand', said the One Minute Manager, 'and I thought to myself, "Well, the session is over. Pack your bags." He said, "I want to say something" and I said, "Go ahead".

'Chris said, "I just want you to know that I use punishment and it works".

'I looked at him and thought to myself, "What are you going to say to someone like Chris?" He could have said that the sky was green and I would have agreed straight away that the sky was green.

'When I regained my composure, I said, "That's interesting, Chris. Would you be willing to tell the others in the group what the advantages of punishment are?"

'He said, "Of course! There are three: it's easy; it's fast; and it makes me feel good."

'Looking at his size, I said to myself, "I'll bet it works for you". Then I said, "If those are the advantages, Chris, are there any drawbacks to using too much punishment?"

'Chris smiled and said, "I can't think of one".

'I said, "I can think of three areas too much punishment can affect – efficiency rates, absenteeism, and staff turnover".

'Chris stared at me because he knew what I was thinking. He had the lowest efficiency rates in the plant. Now he knew that but I had heard his excuses: "I have the toughest department", and "I'm on a swing shift and everyone knows that swing shifts traditionally have the lowest productivity".

'Absenteeism – Chris consistently had 20 per cent of his staff absent so he had eight out of ten at work most days. The personnel people joked that without Chris's department they would have to lay off one staff member. They were busy every day processing transfer requests, resignations, or hiring for his department.

'Staff turnover – his was the highest in the plant. But I had heard him say, "I manage the worst department there is and everyone likes to get out of it as soon as possible".

'When it was obvious I was baiting him, Chris said, "OK, boss. How do you expect me to work differently with the bunch of layabouts I've got working for me? They live to pay for their booze. And besides, I don't like them and they don't like me."

'I said, "Chris, I know you probably think these sessions are a waste of time. But will you give me a chance?"

'"OK!" said Chris. "But I'm not counting on anything."

'After I had talked about the need to start any performance-improvement programme with pinpointing the problem and then recording present performance, I discussed the importance of the daily printout from the computer for checking progress and giving people feedback. You see, in our operation the foremen get good information on performance.'

'As you were speaking, what was Chris doing?' asked the veteran manager.

'He just sat there with his arms crossed', said the One Minute Manager. 'There was no expression on his face.'

'After the meeting, much to my surprise, Chris came up to me and said, "Look, I think this stuff is probably useless, but I'd like to increase my efficiency rate. Any ideas?"

'"Every day you get a printout from the computer on the efficiency of each of your machines for the day before", I replied. "Since you have a one man per machine operation, this information tells you how each of your men is doing. All I want you to do is make a graph for everyone and, at the beginning of every morning, fill in the efficiency ratings on the graphs and then walk around and show each man what his efficiency was from the day before. That's all I want you to do."

'"OK", said Chris. "I'll give it a try even though I don't think it will work."

'The next morning, I went down to see what happened', continued the One Minute Manager. 'Chris got the printout from the computer and transferred the information to graphs for each of his staff and then walked over to his first man and said, "Listen, don't give me any crap about the number on here. Just look at it." And then he showed the man his efficiency rating.

'I thought to myself, "This is going to be a disaster", so I told Chris to simply show them the number and not to say anything else. I told him to say merely "You got 86 per cent efficiency yesterday". "You got 94." "You got 100."

'When he said to the next man, "You got 83 per cent efficiency yesterday", the man said, "Chris, get out of here and get away from me. We're going to call the union. Leave us alone. You've left us alone for years unless we did something wrong, so just get out of here."

'Chris said to me, "I told you they don't like me".

'I said, "Chris, keep trying".

'Chris kept showing his men their efficiency rates even though they were giving him a hard time and not even looking at their graphs. Then after about four days I could see them starting to look when he came along showing them their scores. They were starting to look at the graphs because they were beginning to get feedback and were able to compare how they did yesterday to the day before, and the day before that.'

'And the comparisons were against themselves, not the other men', interrupted the veteran manager.

'Yes', said the One Minute Manager. 'We find it more constructive to have people competing against themselves and a performance standard rather than competing with each other.'

'What happened next?' asked the veteran manager, anxious to get back to hearing about Chris.

'Chris told his staff, "Listen, I'm getting sick and tired of giving this feedback to you all. From now on, if anybody has 85 per cent or higher efficiency, I'll come and show you your rating. But if you didn't get 85 per cent, you don't deserve to talk to me."'

'Let's see if I can fit this story into the PRICE system', suggested the veteran. 'When Chris said he wanted to improve efficiency he was pinpointing the problem. That's *P*. When he made the graphs from the computer printout he was up to *R* for record. And when he began showing his men their efficiency ratings in the beginning he was involving them, even if he was a little autocratic. That's *I*. Now by deciding to talk only with people with 85 per cent or higher efficiency, it sounds as if Chris was beginning to manage consequences and to coach. That's *C*. That decision was made at his own kind of evaluation session: *E*.'

'Exactly!' said the One Minute Manager. 'You really learned the PRICE system quickly, didn't you?'

'I just love the simplicity of it all', said the veteran manager.

'It was funny to see Chris', continued the One Minute Manager, 'walk up to a man and then, reading that his efficiency rate was below 85, walk straight past him without showing him his graph or saying a word. The expression on that person's face was priceless. He acted as if Chris had stabbed him in the back.'

'I bet pretty soon everyone was getting over 85 per cent efficiency', said the veteran manager.

'You're quite right', said the One Minute Manager. 'After a week or so Chris called them all together again. He said, "You've got to achieve 95 per cent efficiency or I don't come to your machine". It was amazing how their efficiency scores climbed.'

'That's amazing, considering that all Chris was doing was giving them the information', said the veteran.

'Right', said the One Minute Manager. 'He didn't say they did well; he didn't say they did badly. Just the fact that Chris would show up at their machines was important to them.

'He did this', continued the One Minute Manager, 'for some time. Then, after about a month, he gave each of them their own graph and stopped coming to their machines but he would leave the printout from the computer on his desk. I swear to you, nine out of ten of the men would run over there during their break time to see what they got and go back and fill in their graphs.'

'Then he started to circle in red the names of those men who got 95 per cent. Can you believe it? A bunch of hard-nosed types like this talking about whether they got a red circle that day. They thought it was really something special if they got a red circle.'

'What was happening to the performance in Chris's department all this time?' asked the veteran manager.

'It was going up like a spaceship on the graph', said the One Minute Manager. 'At the same time his absenteeism and tardiness were going down too. The other foremen didn't believe it. They thought Chris was cheating about the data. I knew he wasn't because I was watching the data all the time.'

'What did he do next?' said the veteran manager.

'One day', said the One Minute Manager, 'he brought all his staff together and said, "You men have really been increasing your efficiency. I'll tell you what I'll do. My wife makes the best chocolate cake you've ever tasted so if everyone in this department gets 100 per cent or higher today, I'll bring in some of her chocolate cake tomorrow for everyone."

'I wasn't at the meeting but I heard about it through the grapevine. I went to see him. I said, "Chris, chocolate cake as a motivator? It's not going to work."

'He said, "That's what you think. Let me do it."

'I said, "Chris, you can do anything you want" – as if I could stop him'.

'Chris didn't even walk around and watch them', continued the One Minute Manager. 'They monitored themselves. For example, the biggest man in the department started walking around and saying things like "Jim, you'd better get 100 per cent". "Joe, you'd better get 100 per cent...." If someone left his machine to get something or do something, one of the men would yell, "Hey, where are you going? You get back to work."'

'Did everyone get 100 per cent efficiency?' asked the veteran manager.

'Too right', said the One Minute Manager. 'No exceptions. So at lunchtime the next day Chris brought in these plates of chocolate cake. You never saw anything go so fast in your life. They loved it.

'I thought that was something, so I decided to try out the idea on the other departments.

'I called in my key staff and told them I would be willing to buy lunch the next day for every department that got 100 per cent or higher in efficiency on any given day'.

'What did your staff think?' asked the veteran manager.

'Everyone thought it was a great idea', said the One Minute Manager. 'We had these little vouchers printed up that the employees could use on the "roach coach".'

'The roach coach?' wondered the veteran manager.

'That's an affectionate name for the food trolley that goes around, selling all kinds of goodies', said the One Minute Manager. 'Our staff often wait to eat lunch until it arrives.'

'While I thought my plan was a good idea, it went down like a lead balloon. In fact, people got hostile. They were saying things like: "This is ridiculous!" "Don't expect us to work ourselves into the ground for a free lunch voucher. We're insulted."'

'What happened?' asked the veteran manager.

'I was confused', said the One Minute Manager, 'so I asked Chris to come and see me'.

'So Chris is now a consultant to top management', laughed the veteran.

'It took courage to admit I needed advice from Chris', confessed the One Minute Manager.

'What did Chris think of the programme?' wondered the veteran manager.

'He had elected not to do the voucher programme', said the One Minute Manager. 'In fact, he was one of the leaders of the revolt. That's why I wanted to talk to him – to find out why he wouldn't participate in the voucher programme.

'When Chris arrived at my office, I asked him, "Why aren't you involved in the voucher programme?"

'Chris leaned over to me and put his finger right in my face and said, "You tried to bribe the employees. You offered them a free voucher on the roach coach to increase productivity. Let me tell you how I and the other men felt about that. We were mad. We felt used and insulted."

'Then he took his finger away from my face, paused, and stared in my eyes for what seemed like an endless moment. "Let me tell you one other thing", Chris said as he broke the silence. "You're good. You've done a tremendous job putting the One Minute Manager to work here. We think you're better than that kind of bribery stuff."

'Then Chris smiled and said, "How's that for a One Minute Reprimand?"

'I have to admit that being on the end of a reprimand from Chris wasn't the most comfortable experience I've ever had', said the One Minute Manager.

'After I got my composure back, I said, "I realise I made a mistake, but how was what I did different from what you did with the chocolate cake?"

'"My wife made that chocolate cake", said Chris. "I put myself out and so did she. You offered to give us a free lunch voucher to use on the roach coach. That's an insult and a bribe."

'"So my lunch voucher", I said, "was insulting because it wasn't personal and it didn't involve any emotional commitment from me?"

'"Right", said Chris. "You have done a fantastic job here, introducing your concepts of One Minute Management and teaching us the ABC's. Most of us are willing to pay the PRICE to get good performance. The people who work for you are winners and you shouldn't take the ball away from them. Don't try to sprinkle reinforcement from on high."

'"I understand what you are saying, Chris", I replied, "and I really want to thank you for your honesty".

'"That's OK", said Chris. "I've learned a lot here and there's no reason why I can't help you learn, too."

'We both smiled and shook hands.'

'Chris is quite a guy, isn't he?' said the veteran manager.

'He certainly is', said the One Minute Manager. 'It's people like him who have really made our efforts worthwhile here.'

'And he's taught me to put the things I've learned here into a human perspective', added the veteran. 'Speaking of the things I've learned, I'd like to sum it all up for you. I want to be certain I've got it all straight.'

'Go ahead', said the One Minute Manager.

'First, I cleared up some questions I had about the three secrets of One Minute Management: One Minute Goal Setting, One Minute Praisings and One Minute Reprimands', remembered the veteran manager. 'Second, I've learned that the ABC's of Management (the Activators, the resulting Behaviour and the appropriate Consequences) help sequence those secrets in a way that makes them usable. And third, the PRICE System gives me a good basic knowledge of how to put the One Minute Manager to work in a systematic way that can be shared with everyone. It turns the secrets into skills and moves the application of One Minute Management beyond individuals to work groups and the organisation as a whole.'

The One Minute Manager smiled as he listened to the veteran. He loved to see the excitement that learning new things sparked in people.

'Sounds as if you have everything pretty straight', commented the One Minute Manager.

'I think I've got it', said the veteran. 'I can't thank you enough for sharing with me what you know and have learned about management.'

'It's my pleasure', said the One Minute Manager. 'All that knowledge is to be shared. Let me leave you with one last thought. The best way to learn to be a One Minute Manager and to use what you have learned is to start to do it. The important thing is not that you do it right, but that you start to do it.'

'I'm really committed to that', said the veteran.

'It's not your commitment that I'm worried about', said the One Minute Manager. 'It's your commitment to your commitment. For example, people say diets don't work. Diets work just fine – it's people who don't work. They break their commitment to their commitment to lose weight. I don't want you to do that with putting the One Minute Manager to work.'

'What you're saying makes sense of what a friend of mine told me', said the veteran. 'He told me I should give up trying. I should either do it or not do it.'

'That's just what I was getting at', said the One Minute Manager. 'To illustrate it, would you try to pick up that pen on the desk?'

The veteran went over to the desk and picked up the pen.

'I told you to try to pick up the pen. I didn't tell you to pick it up', said the One Minute Manager.

The veteran smiled.

'You've got it', said the One Minute Manager. 'You're either going to do it or not going to do it. Saying, "I'll try", just sets up all your past patterns which will result in your not doing it.'

'Thanks for that final advice', said the veteran. 'I certainly don't want to be the man hanging onto the branch on the side of the mountain, yelling, "Is there anybody else up there?"'

With that said, the veteran got up and put his hand out to the One Minute Manager. 'I'm going to do it', he said with sincerity.

WHEN the veteran manager left the One Minute Manager's office, he was excited about implementing what he had learned. He was committed to his commitment to putting the One Minute Manager to work.

The next day he began to do just that. He did not wait until he could do everything he had learned exactly right. He knew if he waited he would never get started, so he shared what he had learned with all his staff, and they in turn shared it with their staff. They all supported one another's efforts to put the secrets of One Minute Management to work.

As he worked with his staff, the veteran manager learned that four systems needed to be set up in the organisation to make One Minute Management pay off. Employees needed to know: what they were being asked to do (accountability system); what good behaviour looked like (performance data system); how well they were doing (feedback system); and what recognition they would get for good performance (recognition system).

Because of his efforts and willingness to share what he had learned, everyone in the veteran manager's organisation set up PRICE projects for each of their One Minute Goals. The goals themselves identified the *pinpointed* areas of interest. Present performance on each of these goals was *recorded*. Then each employee was *involved* in goal setting, as well as establishing coaching and counselling strategies. Then *coaching* began. Managers were responsive to their staff's needs for supervision. Everybody wanted each other to win. When it came to *evaluation* progress was reviewed and new goals set.

Pretty soon the inevitable happened:

The Veteran Manager was Successful In Putting The One Minute Manager To Work And It Made A Difference.

People not only felt better, they performed better. And more importantly, putting the One Minute Manager to work made a difference where it really counted – on the bottom line. Production increased, quality improved, sales skyrocketed, and retention and attendance of employees surpassed all the companies in the area.

Everywhere the veteran manager went he shared what he had learned with others. One Minute Management soon became known as Theory W. The One Minute Manager said, 'You can have your Theory X, Theory Y, and Theory Z. We call One Minute Management "Theory W" because it works.'

Wherever the veteran manager went, he always told people who had learned how to put the One Minute Manager to work . . .

*

*Keep Your
Commitment
To
Your Commitment
And
Share
It
With
Others*

*

About the Authors

Dr. Kenneth H. Blanchard, co-developer of the One Minute Manager and Situational Leadership, is an internationally known author, educator and consultant/trainer, and professor of Leadership and Organisational Behaviour at the University of Massachusetts, Amherst. He has written extensively in the field of leadership, motivation and managing change including the widely used and acclaimed Prentice-Hall text, *Management of Organisational Behaviour: Utilising Human Resources*, co-authored with Paul Hersey and now in its fourth edition, and the national bestseller, *The One Minute Manager* (William Collins) co-authored with Spencer Johnson, M.D

Dr. Blanchard received his B.A. in government and philosophy from Cornell University, an M.A. in sociology and counselling from Colgate University, and a Ph.D. in administration and management from Cornell University.

As chairman of the board of Blanchard Training and Development, Inc., a human resource development company, Dr. Blanchard has trained 50,000 managers and has advised a wide range of corporations and agencies. His approaches to management have been incorporated into many Fortune 500 companies as well as numerous fast-growing entrepreneurial companies.

Dr. Robert L. Lorber, an internationally known and recognised expert in performance improvement, is president of RL Lorber and Associates, Inc., a company specialising in the strategic design and implementation of productivity improvement systems, based in Orange, California.

Dr. Lorber received his B.A. and M.A. degrees from the University of California at Davis and in 1974 was awarded a Ph.D. in Applied Behavioural Science and Organisational Psychology. His numerous publications include *Effective Feedback: The Key to Engineering Performance, Managing Data vs Gut Feeling, How to Implement Change: Supervise and Lead*, and *Productivity – in Five Intensive Lessons*.

Dr. Lorber has spoken at many Young Presidents' Organisation universities and area conferences. He is on the board of the Business School at the University of Santa Clara, the Board of Editors of the *Journal of Organisational Behaviour Management*, The Presidents Association of the American Management Association, the American Productivity Management Association, the American Psychological Association, and the World Affairs Council.

Dr. Lorber and his organisation have implemented productivity systems for small, medium and numerous Fortune 500 companies throughout the United States, as well as the Middle East, South America, Mexico, Africa, Europe, and Canada.

Concept Praisings

We would like to acknowledge and give a public praising to the following people whose conceptual contributions were most valuable to us in the course of preparing this book:

David Berlo for his thoughtful analysis of why organisations are not good places for people to be.

Tom Connellan, *Aubrey Daniels*, and *Larry Miller* for teaching us many things about productivity improvement.

Werner Erhard for what his teachings taught us about making life work and keeping your commitments.

Paul Hersey for being one of the most creative behavioural scientists we know and for his pioneer work on Situational Leadership.

Fred Luthans and *Robert Kreitner* for the first conceptualisation of the ABC's.

Abraham Maslow for the recognition that people's behaviour is driven by different needs at different times.

David McClelland for his pioneer work on achievement motivation and the importance of setting moderately difficult but achievable goals.

Scott Meyers for his outstanding work on understanding and motivating people.

George Odiorne for being 'Mister Management by Objective' (MBO) and for identifying the problems of the 'activity trap'.

B. F. Skinner for his classic work on reinforcement theory.

Rick Tate for his skill in teaching management and coining the phrase 'Feedback Is the Breakfast of Champions'.

The One Minute Manager Meets the Monkey

Kenneth Blanchard
William Oncken, Jr.,
and Hal Burrows

The Symbols

The One Minute Manager's symbol—a one-minute readout from the face of a modern digital watch—is intended to remind each of us to take a minute out of our day to look into the faces of the people we manage. And to realize that they are our most important resources.

The Monkey Manager's symbol—a harried manager overwhelmed by a deskful of problems—is intended to remind us to constantly discipline ourselves to invest our time on the most vital aspects of management rather than dilute our effectiveness by "doing more efficiently those things that shouldn't be done in the first place."

INTRODUCTION

Over a decade ago a real joy came into my life—Bill Oncken. I first came into contact with Bill and his monkey-on-the-back analogy when I was given a copy of his classic November 1974 *Harvard Business Review* article entitled "Managing Management Time: Who's Got the Monkey?" that he co-authored with Donald Wass. I read it and light bulbs began to flash. At the time, I was a tenured full professor in the School of Education at the University of Massachusetts. As such, according to Bill, I was a typical northeastern intellectual bleeding-heart social theorist who thought my role in life was to wipe out pain and suffering by helping everyone. In other words, I was a compulsive monkey-picker-upper.

Then several years later I sat in on one of Bill's "Managing Management Time" seminars. Participants burst into laughter as they recognized the problems Bill discussed. Since crying in public is not an accepted practice, the only thing left for us to do was laugh. And laugh we did. Why? Because Bill Oncken, time after time, hit both the absurdities and realities of organizational life in America with such accuracy that it hurt.

Bill Oncken, more than anyone else, has taught me that if I really want to help others, I need to teach them how to fish rather than give them a fish. Taking the initiative away from people and caring for and feeding their monkeys is nothing more than rescuing them, that is, doing things for them they can do for themselves.

So when Hal Burrows, a longtime associate and principal of the William Oncken Company and one of the outstanding presenters of the "Managing Management Time" seminar, approached me about co-authoring this book, I was thrilled. In fact, I am honored to have this book as part of THE ONE MINUTE MANAGER LIBRARY.

Hal and I wrote several drafts of this book with Bill over about a three-year period. Then Bill suffered a serious illness and died as we were completing the final working draft of this book. So he never saw the finished publication. As I write these words my heart aches because of the loss of Bill. I am especially sad for those people who never knew Bill Oncken, for they suffer the greatest loss. My hope is that reading this book can soften that loss because it reads as accurately and humorously as Bill and colleagues like Hal Burrows have told thousands of managers about monkey management over the years. This is vintage Bill Oncken with the bite and insight left in.

What follows is a story about a harried manager who worked long, hard hours, yet never quite seemed to get caught up with all the work he had to do. He learned about monkey management and how not to take initiative away from his people so they can care for and feed their own "monkeys." In the process, he learned to be more effective in dealing with his own manager and the demands of his organization. The performance of his department drastically improved as did the prospects for his career.

Bill Oncken's seminar and book, "Managing Management Time," include many wonderful insights about how organizations really function and present strategies for gaining the support of your boss, staff, and internal and external peers. The One Minute Manager Meets the Monkey is *adapted from the "staff" strategy.*

My hope is that you will use what you learn in this book to make a difference in your life and the lives of the people you interact with at work and at home.

—Kenneth Blanchard, Ph.D
Co-author
The One Minute Manager

This book is dedicated to the memory of William Oncken, Jr.

Bill Oncken, like Amadeus Mozart, was that exceedingly rare combination of masterful composer and virtuoso performer, the difference being that Bill used words instead of musical notes to fashion his works. His masterwork, *Managing Management Time*, is a timeless, enduring composition that captures the very essence of management, an art as old as organizations themselves. And anyone who ever saw him perform his work will never forget the experience!
—Hal Burrows

Contents

The Problem 13
First Management Position 15
Meeting with Boss 17
Meeting with the One Minute Manager 19
Fundamental Management Dilemma 21
Diagnosis—Self-Inflicted Problem 24
Definition of a Monkey 26
Who Owns the Monkey? 27
Vicious Cycle 33
The Solution 35
The One Minute Manager's Awakening 37
The Depth of the Problem 40
Rescuing 42
A Feeling of Optimism 49
Returning the Monkeys 51
Having Time for My People 54
Oncken's Rules of Monkey Management 58
Rule 1 *Descriptions* 61
Rule 2 *Owners* 67
Rule 3 *Insurance Policies* 78
Rule 4 *Feeding and Checkups* 87
A Summary of Oncken's Four Rules of Monkey Management 94
Delegation 95
Coaching 100
Balancing Three Kinds of Organizational Time 111
Boss-Imposed Time 113

System-Imposed Time 116
Self-Imposed Time 119
Discretionary—The Most Vital Time 120
Starting with Subordinate-Imposed Time 123
Planting Discretionary Time 124
Managing Rather Than Doing 127
The Ultimate Conversion 129

Praisings 132
About the Authors 134
Services Available 137

IF you are someone who feels overwhelmed with problems created by other people, what you are about to read can change your life. It's the story of a manager, but it applies as well to other roles in life, especially parents and teachers.

This is the account of how my career went from imminent failure to considerable success after some wise counsel from two able people. My purpose in telling it here is to pass along their wisdom to you in the hope that it will help you as it has helped me.

The story begins some two years ago after a luncheon meeting with my friend, the One Minute Manager. I returned to my office, sat down at my desk, shook my head in amazement, and thought about what had just happened.

During lunch I had poured out my frustrations about my work. My friend listened and then told me the cause of my problems. I was astonished that the solution was so obvious.

What surprised me most was that the problem was self-inflicted. I guess that's why I couldn't see it without some help. But when my eyes were opened I realized that I was not alone; I knew other managers with the same problem.

As I sat there alone in my office I laughed aloud. "Monkeys!" I said to no one in particular. "I never would have suspected my problem is monkeys."

For the first time in a long time I remember smiling as I glanced at the picture on my desk of my wife and children. I began to look forward to enjoying more time with them.

About a year before the "monkey revelation" I had been appointed to my first management position. Things had started off well. I was initially very enthusiastic about my new work, and my attitude seemed to rub off on the people who reported to me. Productivity and morale gradually increased; both had been reported to be low before I took over as head of the department.

After the initial surge, however, the output of the department began to decline, slowly at first, then rapidly. The drop in performance was followed by a similar slide in morale. Despite long hours and hard work, I was unable to arrest the decline in my department. I was puzzled and very frustrated; it seemed that the harder I worked, the further behind I got and the worse the performance of my department became.

I was working extra hours every workday as well as Saturdays and some Sundays. I just never got caught up. There was pressure every minute, and it was extremely frustrating. I feared I was developing an ulcer and a nervous twitch!

I realized that all this was starting to wear a little thin with my family, too. I was so seldom home that my wife, Sarah, had to manage most of the family problems alone. And when I was home, I was usually tired and preoccupied with work, sometimes even in the middle of the night. Our two kids were also disappointed because I never seemed to have any time to play with them. But I didn't see any alternatives. After all, I had to get the work done.

My boss, Alice Kelley, had not been initially critical of me, but I began to notice a change in her behavior. She started asking for more reports on the performance of my department. She was obviously starting to watch things more closely.

ALICE seemed to appreciate the fact that I wasn't knocking on her door all the time asking for help. But at the same time she was more than a little concerned about the performance of my department. I knew I could not let things go on like that much longer. Consequently, I made an appointment to see her.

I told her I knew things had not been going well lately but I hadn't yet figured out how to improve the situation. I remember telling her my workload made me feel as if I were doing the work of two people. I'll never forget her reply: "Tell me who they are and I'll see that one of them is fired because I can't afford the overhead."

Then she asked me if perhaps I shouldn't be turning over more to my staff. My answer was that my staff was not ready to take on the additional responsibility. Again she responded in a way I'll never forget: "Then it's your job to get them ready! This situation is making me very nervous, and as Benjamin Franklin's grandfather once said:"

*

*It's Tough
To Work For
A Nervous Boss,
Especially
If You Are The One
Who's Making Your Boss
Nervous!*

*

AFTER my meeting with Alice, I thought a lot about what she had said. Those words "nervous boss" kept coming back to me. I began to realize that Alice was expecting me to handle this situation on my own, probably because she was extremely busy herself on a critical project. That's why I had called the One Minute Manager for help. He was a senior manager in another company and a longtime family friend. Everyone called him the "One Minute Manager" because he got such great results from his people with seemingly little time and effort on his part.

When we met at lunch, my problems must have shown on my face because the first thing he said was "So, being a manager is not as easy as you thought, eh?"

"That's an understatement," I answered. I lamented that back in the good old days before I became a manager things were a lot easier because my performance depended strictly on my own efforts. In those days, the longer and harder I worked the more I got done. "That formula seems to be working in reverse now," I told him.

As I went on to describe my problem in greater detail, the One Minute Manager just listened, only breaking his silence with an occasional question. His questions got more and more specific as the conversation continued. He asked me which aspect of my work was taking the biggest portion of my time.

I told him about an avalanche of paperwork in my office. "It's horrendous and getting worse." Sometimes it seemed that all I did was shuffle papers without ever making any progress on the real work that needed to be done; I labeled it *the triumph of technique over purpose*. It was a paradox—I was doing more but accomplishing less.

It seemed that everyone in the company needed something from me yesterday, things that might have been important to them but had little to do with getting my job done. And when I tried to focus on one matter, I would inevitably be interrupted to attend to another. I was spending more time in meetings and on the telephone. By the time I took care of all the paperwork, meetings, and interruptions, there was just no time left to implement some of the ideas I had for improving our own operation.

I told him I had even taken a seminar on time management. Frankly, I think the course made things worse. In the first place, attending it got me two days farther behind in my work. Moreover, even though it helped me become a bit more efficient, I think my increased efficiency merely made room for more work because no matter how much I did there was always more to do.

Then there was my staff. Wherever I saw them—in hallways, elevators, parking lots, cafeteria lines—there was always something they needed from me before they could proceed with their work; I guess that's why I had to work overtime and they didn't. If I left my office door open they were constantly streaming in, so I usually kept it closed. I regretted doing that because I was holding up their work and I suspected that was a big part of their morale problem.

The One Minute Manager listened carefully to my tale of woe. When I finally finished, he suggested that I seemed to be the victim of a fundamental management dilemma:

*Why Is It
That Some Managers
Are Typically
Running Out Of Time
While Their Staffs
Are Typically
Running Out Of Work?*

*

I thought that was an excellent question, particularly when I added up all the people in addition to my staff who were vying for my time. "But," I remarked, "perhaps I shouldn't complain about people needing me all the time. The way things have been going lately, being indispensable might be my only job security!"

The One Minute Manager disagreed sharply. He explained that indispensable managers can be harmful, not valuable, especially when they impede the work of others. Individuals who think they are irreplaceable because they are indispensable tend to get replaced because of the harm they cause. Moreover, higher management cannot risk promoting people who are indispensable in their current jobs because they have not trained a successor.

His explanation sent my thoughts back to my last conversation with my boss, who certainly didn't act as though I was indispensable. In fact, the more I thought about it, the more I realized that if I didn't soon resolve my problems our next conversation could be about career planning . . . for me! And why not? If I could not manage even my current small department, perhaps I shouldn't even be a manager.

IT was at that point during lunch that the One Minute Manager bowled me over with his astonishing (to me!) diagnosis of my problem. First he suggested that my attempts to solve the problem—working overtime, attending seminars—addressed merely the symptoms of the problem, not the cause itself. He said it was like taking an aspirin to reduce the fever but ignoring the illness that caused the fever. As a result, the problem had gotten progressively worse.

I remember thinking, "This is not what I want to hear, that all the work I've been doing has made the problem worse. After all, if I hadn't done the work I would be even farther behind."

I objected to my friend's diagnosis, but my argument soon fell by the wayside when his probing turned up the fact that the mission and staff of my department had not changed since my arrival—the only change *was* my arrival! An unsettling reality suddenly pried its way into my mind. To paraphrase Pogo, "I have seen the enemy, and he is I!"

Remembering that moment I often think about the story of a group of workers having lunch. They all had lunch boxes. One, when he opened his box and saw the contents, shouted, "Bologna sandwiches again! This is the fourth straight day I've had bologna sandwiches. And I don't like bologna!"

One of his co-workers said, "Relax! Relax! Why don't you ask your wife to pack some other kind of sandwich?"

"My wife, heck!" the worker said. "I made the sandwiches myself."

Since there seemed to be nowhere else to look for the source of the problem, I asked my friend to tell me more. He looked me straight in the eye and said, "Your problem is . . . MONKEYS!"

"Monkeys!" I laughed. "That sounds about right. My office usually seems like a zoo. What do you mean?" Then he gave me this definition of a monkey:

*

A Monkey
Is The Next Move

*

Who Owns the Monkey? / 27

HE explained the definition with an example so vivid and true to life that I can quote it to you almost word for word to this day.

> Let's say I am walking down the hall when I encounter one of my people, who says, "Good morning, boss. Can I see you for a minute? We have a problem." I need to be aware of my people's problems so I stand there in the hallway listening while he explains the problem in some detail. I get sucked into the middle of it, and, because problem-solving is my cup of tea, time flies. When I finally glance at my watch, what seemed like five minutes has actually been thirty.
>
> The discussion has made me late for where I was headed. I know just enough about the problem to know I will have to be involved, but not yet enough to make a decision. So I say, "This is a very important problem, but I don't have any more time to discuss it right now. Let me think about it and I'll get back to you." And with that, the two of us part company.

"As a detached, perceptive observer," he continued, "it was probably easy for you to see what happened in that scenario. I assure you it is much harder to see the picture when you are in the middle of it. Before the two of us met in the hall the monkey was on my staff member's back. While we were talking, the matter was under joint consideration, so the monkey had one leg on each of our backs. But when I said, 'Let me think it over and get back to you,' the monkey moved its leg from my subordinate's back onto my back and my subordinate walked away thirty pounds lighter. Why? Because the monkey then had both legs on my back.

"Now, let us assume for the moment that the matter under consideration was part of my staff member's job. And let us further assume that he was perfectly capable of bringing along some proposed solutions to accompany the problem he raised. That being the case, when I allowed that monkey to leap onto my back I volunteered to do two things a person working for me is generally expected to do: (1) I accepted the responsibility for the problem from the person, and (2) I promised the person a progress report. Let me explain:

*

*For
Every Monkey
There Are Two
Parties Involved:
One To Work It
And One To Supervise It*

*

"In the instance just described, you can see that I acquired the worker role and my subordinate assumed the supervisory role. And just to make sure I know who's the new boss, the next day he will stop by my office several times to say, 'Hi, boss. How's it coming?' And if I have not resolved the matter to his satisfaction, he will suddenly be pressuring me to do what is actually his job."

I was dumbfounded. The One Minute Manager's vivid description of role reversal instantly triggered pictures in my mind of dozens of monkeys currently residing in my own office.

The most recent was a memo from Ben, a member of my staff, that said, in effect, "Boss, we're not getting the support we need from Purchasing on the Beta Project. Could you speak to their manager about it?" And, of course, I agreed. Since that time Ben had twice followed up on the matter with "How's it coming on the Beta Project? Have you spoken with Purchasing yet?" Both times I guiltily replied, "Not yet, but don't worry, I will."

Another was from Maria, who was requesting my help because I possessed (as she so astutely observed) "greater knowledge of the organization and of the technical peculiarities of certain problems" than she did.

Yet another monkey I had promised to handle was to write a job description for Erik, who had been transferred from another department to fill a newly created position in my department. I had not had time to specify exactly the duties of this new job, so when he asked me what was expected of him, I promised to write a job description to clarify his responsibilities.

My mind raced with a blur of monkeys and how I had acquired them. Two recent monkeys were in the form of incomplete staff work from Leesa and Gordon. I was planning to analyze the one from Leesa, note the areas that needed more work, and return it to her with suggested changes. The other, from Gordon, was back in my office for the fourth time; I was thinking of completing it myself rather than having to deal with him again.

Monkeys, monkeys, monkeys! I even had some *ricochet monkeys!* These monkeys were created by Maria, whose work and personal style sometimes caused problems for people in other parts of the organization. The other people then brought the problems to me for my invariable reply: "I'll look into it and get back to you."

As I thought about it, I realized that some of the monkeys were opportunities rather than problems. For example, Ben is a very creative person who is great at conceiving new ideas. But, to put it mildly, developing his ideas into finished products is not one of his strengths. So he sent me a series of suggestions which, though underdeveloped, had so much potential that I penned myself notes of things to do in order to capitalize on each of them.

As monkey after monkey scampered through my mind, I clearly saw that most of them should have been handled by my staff. But some of the monkeys belonged to me alone; that is, they were part of *my* job description. For example, when one of my people is sick or untrained or otherwise incapable of doing a task, I sometimes have to help out. And when emergencies arise, I sometimes handle monkeys my staff should handle if there were no emergency. Another example of monkeys that legitimately belong to me is the case where a member of my staff formulates a recommendation for handling a particular situation. Once that person gives the recommendation to me, then one or more of several "next moves" legitimately belong to me. I need to read the recommendation or listen to it being explained, question it, think about it, make a decision, react to it, and so on.

THE One Minute Manager confirmed my observation that some monkeys belong to me, but we both agreed, however, that by far the greatest proportion of the monkeys in my office at that time were those I should never have picked up.

You can easily imagine how this becomes a vicious cycle. When I picked up monkeys my people could have handled, they got the message that I *wanted* the monkeys. So naturally the more I picked up, the more they gave me. Soon I had as many as I could handle in a normal workday (given all the other requirements of my job from my boss and others), but the monkeys kept coming.

So I began "borrowing" time from my personal life: exercise, hobbies, civic activities, church, and eventually from my family. (I rationalized, "It's the quality, not the quantity, of the time with them that counts.")

I eventually reached the point where there was no more time available. But the monkeys still kept coming. That's when I started procrastinating. I was procrastinating and my staff was waiting. We were both doing nothing on the monkeys, a costly duplication of effort!

My procrastination made me a bottleneck to my staff; immobilized by me, they became bottlenecks to people in other departments. When those people complained to me, I would promise to look into the matters and get back to them. Time spent on these "sideward-leaping monkeys" reduced the amount of time for my staff's monkeys even more. Then my boss got wind that there might be problems in my department and started demanding more reports from me. These "downward-leaping monkeys" took precedence over all others, and time spent on them left even less time for the others. Looking back on that mess, I realize I was the cause of organizational gridlock; it is incredible how much trouble I caused.

Of course, the greater problem was that of "opportunity cost"; spending *all* my time working on other people's monkeys meant I had no opportunity to work on my own. I was not manag*ing*, I was being manag*ed*. I was not *pro*active, I was strictly *re*active. I was merely coping.

As we continued our lunch, the One Minute Manager and I talked mostly about the problems monkeys create in organizations. We were almost finished before it dawned on me that I was not at all sure what to do about this monkey business, so I confessed, "I admit it. I do have a huge menagerie of my staff's monkeys. But what can I do about it? And what can I do about the problems with my boss, and about the time-consuming demands of all the other people in the organization?"

He replied, "Many of those downward-leaping monkeys from your boss and those sideward-leaping monkeys from your peers are offspring of the upward-leaping monkeys from your staff. Once you correct this situation with your staff you'll have time to deal with those other two sets of monkeys. But this is not the time or place to discuss that process. The best way to learn about that is by attending a seminar called "Managing Management Time."

I reminded him that I had already taken a time-management course and the course only made things worse.

"Ah," he said, "but this seminar is different. The course you took focused on doing things right, which is okay, but it neglected to teach you the right things to do. You became more efficient, but you were doing the wrong things. You were like a pilot making great landings at the wrong airport. The seminar I'm recommending will help you learn:"

*

*Things
Not Worth
Doing
Are Not
Worth Doing
Well*

*

As we were leaving the restaurant I thanked the One Minute Manager for his help and promised I would make every effort to attend the seminar (secretly wondering how I could possibly take two days off from work!). Then I got the shock of my life when I asked him how he happened to know so much about this monkey management.

Grinning, the One Minute Manager answered, "Because I once had the same problem you do, only much, much worse. Like you, my career was in trouble and I was desperate. One day a brochure announcing a time-management seminar came across my desk. Like a drowning man grasping for a straw I decided to attend. It was lucky I did because that's where I learned all about monkey management!"

It was hard for me to believe that such a professional manager could ever have suffered from this problem. I asked him to tell me more, and the One Minute Manager did, with gusto.

"The course was taught by its creator, Bill Oncken. I'll never forget the spellbinding story he told that opened my eyes to the problem. It was a parable that paralleled my situation so closely it was eerie.

"Oncken told us how, like you and me, he'd been working long hours but still couldn't keep up. And how, as usual, he left home early one Saturday morning to go to work to get caught up, explaining to his disappointed wife and kids that his sacrifice was all for them. I almost cried when I heard him say that because I had uttered those very words the previous weekend.

"Oncken told us how he looked out his office window that Saturday morning to the golf course across the street and saw his staff there, getting ready to tee off. 'They were teeing up,' he said, 'and I was teed off! I became convinced that if, by magic, I could be transformed into a fly and buzz about their heads, I would overhear one of them remark to another: "Things are looking up, did you see whose car just pulled into the company parking lot? Looks like the boss has finally decided to earn his money!"'"

The One Minute Manager continued, "Then Oncken told us he looked down at that pile of papers on his desk and suddenly realized this was *their* work he was about to do. He was behind in their work, not his. He had never been behind in his work because he never had gotten it started! Then it hit him like a thunderbolt—'They're not working for me; I'm working for them! And with four of them generating work and only one of me working it off, I'll never get caught up by working harder because the more I do, the more they will give me!'

"Then," continued the One Minute Manager, obviously enjoying telling the story, "Oncken said, 'It suddenly hit me that I was way behind in some other things as well. So I ran out of my office and down the hall as fast as my legs would carry me. The weekend janitor, seeing me go by like a streak of lightning, asked where I was going in such a hurry. I yelled back that my speed was explained by where I was leaving from, not where I was going to.'

"Mr. Oncken related how he went down the stairs hitting every sixth step, jumped in his car and sped home. In the space of half an hour he had gone from the agony of facing two days of work to the thrill of spending two days with his family. He had a great weekend with his family and Saturday night he slept so soundly that twice during the night his wife thought he was dead.

"Yes," said the One Minute Manager, "Bill Oncken painted a perfect picture of me, a compulsive monkey-picker-upper. But thank goodness he showed us what to do about it, and my life has never been the same since. Nor will yours."

"I'll bet I know the title of the seminar you attended," I said. My friend smiled and nodded his agreement.

AFTER we parted, amazed at all I had heard, I returned to my office. When I walked in I saw monkeys everywhere. Where I had once seen backs of envelopes with notes written to myself, I now saw monkeys. (I have since given some thought to going into business selling pads of "backs of envelopes" to people like me.) Telephone messages were monkeys. (I pictured a monkey going through a telephone line like a pig passing through a python.) My briefcase appeared as a monkey cage. The note pad on my desk was a grappling hook, which I had so often used to pull monkeys off other people's backs.

As I looked around my office that day, my gaze settled on the picture of my wife and children and for the first time ever I realized *I have never been in the picture!* I resolved to correct that.

The family picture also reminded me that my wife and I pick up our kids' monkeys. Just recently my son came home and said to us, "Mom! Dad! I made the junior tennis team!"

We said, "Great! Isn't that wonderful. We're proud of you." Then he said, "There's only one problem: I need a ride to practice after school every Monday, Wednesday, and Friday, and then someone needs to pick me up when we're done." And who do you think got that monkey? My wife and I. What started as a celebration became a monkey.

What's worse is that the monkey quickly multiplied! My wife said to my son, "I could take you on Monday and some Fridays, but Wednesdays are a real problem for me. Who else is on your team so maybe I can set up a car pool?"

After my son told her who was on the team, she said, "I'll get on this right away, honey, and let you know who will be driving you." Without a care in the world, my son ran off to watch TV with a cheery, "Thanks, Mom."

OF course my son couldn't drive a car, but he certainly could have made an effort to arrange transportation alternatives and in the process learned to take some responsibility. Reliving that situation made me realize how easily we needlessly pick up other people's monkeys in all arenas of life. In the process, we neglect our own monkeys and make other people dependent upon us and deprive them of opportunities to learn to solve their own problems.

In retrospect, I can better understand the statements of General George C. Marshall, who said, "If you want someone to be for you, never let him feel he is dependent on you. Make him feel that you are in some way dependent on him," and Benjamin Franklin, who said, "The best way to convert a friend into an enemy is to get him indebted to you."

As I reviewed my luncheon discussion with the One Minute Manager, I realized he was concerned that I had become a "rescuer"—someone who was doing for others what they could do for themselves and in the process giving them the message they were "not okay." He told me that every time one of my people came to me and shared a problem and I took the monkey away from that person, what I was saying, in essence, was "You're not capable of handling this problem so I had better take care of it myself."

The One Minute Manager said that I was by no means alone in what I was doing. In fact, he implied it was almost becoming a disease in our country. He even had contemplated starting an organization called "Rescuers Anonymous" for people who were compulsive monkey-picker-uppers. It would be a gathering of "do-gooders"— very loving people who were running around trying to help others but who were crippling those they were trying to help by making them dependent. He said we have almost institutionalized rescuing in our government and throughout our society.

Then the One Minute Manager illustrated the depths of the rescuing mentality in this country by telling me his example of Little League. I can almost hear him now:

"When I was young, if we wanted to play baseball we had three problems. First of all, we needed equipment. In those days the one thing that guaranteed you would play was having a bat. There just weren't that many bats available then and if your bat broke, you'd never even think about running home and asking your parents to buy you a new one. Instead, you'd pound a few nails in it and wrap it with tape. I'll never forget running down to first base with my hands vibrating from one of those 'broken bats.'

"I also didn't know a baseball was white until I was nine—that's when we got our first TV. All the balls we used were covered with black tape. In fact, sometimes with a large ball you didn't know whether it was a softball or really a hardball that just had so much tape around it that it was the size of a softball. I just knew that some of the balls were so heavy that if you could hit a fly ball to the shortstop that was considered a 'long hit.'

"And gloves?" The One Minute Manager continued, "We didn't have that many then and I wasn't from a poor neighborhood. I can never remember running in from the field to bat when I didn't throw my glove to someone coming out to field. Today I know kids who have two or three different gloves.

"Once we got our equipment, the second problem was finding a place to play. If you lived in the city, you'd find a city block that didn't get much traffic and where residents could park their cars elsewhere. Then you would use the sewers, hydrants and the like for bases. If you lived in the country, as I did, you found a vacant lot or a farmer's field where you could clear off all the rocks except the four you were going to use for bases.

"The third and last problem, once we had equipment and a field," said the One Minute Manager, "was to find kids to play. Since we rarely had an abundance of kids, we had to choose from what was available. As a result, a team would range in age all the way from seven or eight to eighteen. I had real heroes when I was a kid. I remember that if Harry Haig even said 'hello' to me when I was a kid, I was thrilled. If he asked me to go to right field on defense, I never complained. Not even when a left-handed batter came up and he shouted for me to get in left field! I never ran home and told my parents I wasn't playing enough. I just knew if I was patient, when I got older I would get to pitch, catch, or play third base.

"After we had equipment, a field, and kids, we started hitting the ball around and playing choose-up games. Pretty soon we started thinking we were real good. Then someone would say, 'I understand Keith Dollar has a group that plays ball in his neighborhood.' So someone would see Dollar in school and challenge his team to a game. We'd play and beat them and then someone else would say, 'I understand Bill Bush has a group.' So we'd challenge them and beat 'em.

"We ended up having a six-team league when I was a kid: the Berrian Bombers, the Seacord Sissies, the Abafoil Asses and others like them. But who did all the planning? We did! Who did all the organizing? We did! And the motivating and controlling? We did!" exclaimed the One Minute Manager.

"And who does it today? The parents! All the kids have to do is get dressed. And do they get dressed! They all look like Joe DiMaggio or Willie Mays. And it's not just baseball—it's all youth sports. I remember working with a top manager in a Canadian company last year. In the middle of the afternoon he asked if I minded taking a drive with him to pick up his son so he could take him to youth hockey. We drove to his home and tooted the horn. The door opened and a kid came staggering out just loaded down with equipment. He was obviously a goalie. I asked, 'How old is he?,' since I couldn't tell.

"'Seven' was the answer. Halfway down the sidewalk the kid tripped and fell. If we hadn't gotten out of the car and helped him up he would have died there. With all that equipment on, there was no way he could have gotten up himself.

"I remember playing hockey as a kid on the lake in front of the high school," said the One Minute Manager. "We would spend all afternoon clearing the snow off the lake. Then, just about the time we finished and we were ready to play, our moms would come by and tell us to come home for dinner. That night it would snow again and we'd have to start clearing again the next day. When we finally got the ice cleared, we'd put two rocks at either end of our 'rink' to mark the goals. And if you played goalie then, and even hinted that you were wearing a 'jock,' they would call you a 'sissy.'

"After the kids get dressed today they get driven to the games. No one would want them to get any exercise. Once they get to the game, there are incredible fields with a refreshment stand where mothers and fathers are sweating, preparing hot dogs and hamburgers and all kinds of goodies. We certainly wouldn't want the kids to be hungry!

"Then there are parents sitting in the stands with major-league scorebooks scoring the game. When a kid hits one to third and the fielder throws him out, the poor parent has to figure what to write down as if this was the World Series.

"In the outfield there is a kid, sweating like mad, changing the scoreboard. When we were kids we kept score on the ground with a stick. One of the opponents would come over and say, 'You didn't get that run,' and would rub it out with his foot. Then you'd have to push him aside and scratch it in again.

"And the final straw," said the One Minute Manager, "when the game is over today and you lose, you can't even hassle the opponent! You have to go to Baskin-Robbins or Häagen-Dazs for ice cream. Have you ever tried to get ice cream on a Saturday afternoon? Every kid in town is in there, legions of little future major leaguers, yelling for some ice cream.

"As parents we have taken all the 'next moves' away from our kids. As a result, all the monkeys are on our backs, and the kids don't learn responsibility. In our well-intentioned desire to give them the good things we didn't have, we sometimes neglect to give them the good things we did have. Often kids today don't know what to do if nothing is planned," emphasized the One Minute Manager. "When I was a kid, if I told my mother I was bored, she would either give me a good swift kick in the pants and say, 'How's that for a little excitement?,' or say, 'That's great! Go clean out the garage.' We'd sure get over our boredom quickly."

A Feeling of Optimism / 49

WHAT I began to learn from the One Minute Manager, and continued to learn from the seminar he recommended was that the more I take care of everything for other people, the more dependent they become. In the process, their self-esteem and confidence are eroded and I am prevented from dealing effectively with my own monkeys.

Many of the monkeys in my office (mine and my staff's) were pitifully emaciated for lack of attention. I figuratively patted one of my staff's monkeys on the head and said, "Don't worry, little fellow, you'll be going home soon." Then with a glance at my own monkeys I said, "And I will finally have some time for you!"

A feeling of optimism came over me as I glanced up to my office wall at the poster my wife had given me some years ago. It showed a picture of Sir Isaac Newton sitting under a tree, having just been bopped on the head by a falling apple. The caption read:

*Experience
Is Not
What Happens
To You;
It's What
You Do
With
What Happens
To You*

*

Returning the Monkeys / 51

As I sat there in my office that Friday after lunch, I knew my life had just taken a sharp turn for the better. At the same time I had a sneaking suspicion that there was a lot more to learn. Nevertheless, I left my office early that day to enjoy a rare delightful weekend with my family. In fact, my minister expressed surprise at seeing me in church on an "off Sunday," which he explained was all except Easter. In the past he would always say on Easter Sunday, "Let me be the first to wish you a Merry Christmas!"

At this point I suppose you are wondering what happened to all those monkeys when I returned to my office on Monday morning after the weekend with my family. Very little, as it turned out, because, first, I didn't know what to do about them, and second, I spent the first three days of the week scrambling to get things arranged so I could attend the seminar the One Minute Manager recommended.

And attend I did! The "Managing Management Time" seminar was just as eye-opening an experience as the One Minute Manager said it would be. What I liked about it most was you could put what you learned into practice right away. I couldn't wait until the Monday after the seminar. That's when all the monkeys got what they deserved. I can assure you it was a day my staff and I will not soon forget.

As I drove to work that day, my mind was filled with delicious anticipation as I thought over the strategies and techniques I was about to apply with my staff. I could hardly wait to return my people's monkeys to their proper owners.

Heavy traffic that morning caused me to arrive about ten minutes late at my office, which was just enough time for my staff to assemble outside where they often performed their supervisory duties of checking on their monkeys.

As I walked past them into my office, both they and I sensed a profound change in the air. I, because I knew what was about to happen, and they because the smile on my face told them they didn't. They had never seen me smile like that on Monday morning. That sudden change in my behavior made them burp in chorus. (Sudden, drastic changes can make people nervous!)

I was smiling because I saw them in an entirely new light! I had long viewed them as a major *source* of my problems; suddenly that morning, I saw them as the major *solution* to my problem. I saw each of their backs as a repository for several monkeys.

As I walked into my office, Valerie, my secretary, saw me forget to do something I had not forgotten to do in years. I forgot to shut my door. That made *her* burp! (Please note that without speaking a word I had upset my entire staff!) When I shouted out to ask Valerie who was first to see me, she couldn't believe her ears. "You mean you actually want to see somebody?" she asked. Replied I, "I never wanted to see somebody so badly in all my life. Who's first?"

At that point, following the sequence recommended by our seminar instructor, I took the first step toward my recovery—getting rid of my people's monkeys. Over the course of the morning I met with each member of my staff and followed virtually the same procedure with each. First I apologized for having been a bottleneck to them, and I promised them that things would never again be the same.

54 / Having Time for My People

THEN I firmly attached my people's monkeys to *their* backs and sat back and enjoyed an exhilarating sight as each subordinate departed my office . . . several monkeys screwed squarely between the shoulder blades of their departing owner! And later that day I made it a point to ask each of my people the same question all of them had been asking me for so long: "How's it coming?" (This is "job enrichment" for managers!)

When the last of them left my office that morning I sat there, alone, reflecting on the things that had just come to pass. The most obvious was that my door was open for a change; even so, there were no people or monkeys in there with me. I had achieved privacy and accessibility at the same time! For the first time in a long time I had time for my people but they didn't have time for me. What an important learning:

*The More You
Get Rid Of
Your People's
Monkeys,
The More Time
You Have For
Your People*

That point was driven home by an incident that occurred a couple of days after the Monday when my people got all their monkeys back. I was in my office, alone, with the door open and my feet on my desk, thinking. I was thinking about the things I could do to clear the way so my people could do their things. (In a very real sense, I was working for them, but I was not doing their work!) At the same time, my people were working on their monkeys and I hadn't seen them in a couple of days. Frankly, I was lonely! I didn't feel needed anymore.

As luck would have it, just then Erik came to see me about a problem. As he approached my office he noticed that my door was open. But from where he was standing he couldn't see me in there. Never had he seen my door open when I was in my office, so he must have assumed I was away on a trip. When he asked Valerie where I was, she said, "He's right in there." Erik was so shocked he stammered, "Well, uh, when could I see him?" Valerie replied, "Just go right on in. He's just sitting there. He isn't doing anything!"

When he came in I realized how lonely I had been. I greeted him warmly: "Come on in. Have a seat. I'm so glad to see you. How about some coffee? Let's start at the beginning. How are your wife and kids these days?" Erik's reply told me that my greeting was perhaps a bit more effusive and time-consuming than he felt was called for under the circumstances. Shaking his head he said, "I don't have time for that kind of B.S.!" *For once I had more time for him than he had for me!*

My staff knew, as does anyone who's ever experienced it, how frustrating it is to work for a boss who has no time for them. So now I endeavor always to have more time for them than they have for me. That is accomplished by expanding the amount of time I have for them and contracting the amount of time they have for me. I keep tabs on how I'm doing in this regard by always noting who runs out of time first each time I meet with a member of my staff; if they are running out of time more often than I am, that's a good indicator of their increasing self-reliance.

Consequently, I have developed the reputation among my staff as the most accessible manager they have ever known. They can see me as often as they wish (which is not very often) and for as long as they wish (which is not very long). This is a vast change from the time before my "conversion."

MOREOVER, once my people regained control of their monkeys that Monday, they were empowered to act. Thus they were no longer frustrated waiting for *me* to act, nor was I guilty because I owed them responses that I didn't have time to make. I was no longer an impediment to them as when I had their monkeys stacked in my office. In the space of a few hours I had gone from being indispensable (that is, my people couldn't make a move until I did) to being dispensable. As I learned, indispensable bosses are dangerous to organizations; thus they tend to get replaced. But bosses who are not impediments to their people can die and not even be missed, and bosses who can die and not be missed are so rare they are virtually irreplaceable. Why?

As a manager, to the extent that you can get people to care for and feed their own monkeys, they are really managing the work themselves. That frees up your discretionary time to do planning, coordinating, innovating, staffing, and other key managerial tasks that will keep your unit functioning well into the future.

Now, having gotten this far on Monday, let's put matters into the proper perspective. What I have done so far is return my people's monkeys to them in accordance with Oncken's Rules of Monkey Management. Now let me tell you all about those rules!

Oncken's Rules of Monkey Management

The dialogue between a boss and one of his or her people must not end until all monkeys have:

Rule 1. *Descriptions:*
The "next moves" are specified.

Rule 2. *Owners:*
The monkey is assigned to a person.

Rule 3. *Insurance Policies:*
The risk is covered.

Rule 4. *Monkey Feeding and Checkup Appointments:*
The time and place for follow-up is specified.

The purpose of the rules of monkey management is to help ensure that the *right things* get done the *right way* at the *right time* by the *right people*.

Monkey rules are crucial if you think back to some of the problem-solving meetings you've attended. Most of those meetings ended without everyone in the room agreeing *what* the "next moves" were to be, *when* they were to be made, and *who* was responsible for making them.

The problem with such meetings is that if no one knows what the "next move" is, it can't be made. Also, if no one has been assigned responsibility for it, then it becomes everybody's responsibility (or rather, nobody's responsibility), which raises the odds nothing will be done. And even if a "next move" is specified and assigned to someone, if there is no deadline attached, the odds of procrastination are increased because we are all too busy with urgent matters to spend time on matters that can be put off.

The rules of monkey management should be applied only to monkeys that deserve to live. Some do not. Some monkeys are in the same category as the British civil-service job that consisted of standing atop the white cliffs of Dover and ringing a bell if Napoleon's troops started across the English Channel—a job that was filled until 1948. So always ask yourself: "Why are we doing this?" If there is no viable answer, shoot the monkey so that you won't be doing more efficiently things that should not be done in the first place.

Rule 1 *Descriptions* / 61

IN order to understand and apply the rules of monkey management, it will help to bear in mind the definition of a monkey. Remember, the monkey is not a project or a problem; *the monkey is whatever the "next move" is* on a project or problem.

Rule 1 means that *a boss and a staff member shall not part company until appropriate "next moves" have been described*. Some examples of monkey descriptions are: "Obtain final cost figures from accounting," "Prepare a sales proposal," "Give the matter further thought," "Formulate a recommendation," and "Get the contract signed."

There are three principal benefits of adhering to this rule. First of all, if my people know in advance that the dialogue between them and me will not end until appropriate "next moves" have been described, they will tend to do *more careful planning before our dialogue begins*. My boss, Alice, taught me this lesson long ago. One day I was bending her ear about all my problems, and I asked her what I should do. She said, "You mean you don't know what to do?" I told her I didn't, so she said, "Well, I don't know what you should do, either. That makes two of us who don't know what you should do, and the company can afford only one of us!"

That was her way of reminding me that for every problem or opportunity brought to her attention, I should also bring some thoughtful recommendations for the "next moves" to be made on the situation. That way we wouldn't have to stand there in the hallway and do the thinking that I should have done before we talked.

The second benefit of Rule 1 is that it *biases any situation toward action by your people*. Many situations are biased toward paralysis, and no progress can be made until someone makes a "next move." For instance, when a problem or opportunity first arises, often the best solution is not immediately apparent, and often the potential hazards of the situation are not obvious. In those cases (especially if there is a lot at stake) it's so tempting for a boss to protect himself or herself by grabbing the monkey.... "Let me think about it and I'll get back to you." That leaves the staff member and the entire project on hold until the boss takes action; the person's initiative has been taken away by the boss. On the other hand, if the "next moves" are clearly described during the dialogue, it often becomes apparent that the subordinate can safely handle many of them, for example, "Give the matter some thought and study" and/or "Formulate a recommendation based on what is known to date." That way the situation doesn't stay in limbo until the boss gets around to doing something about it.

The third and probably the greatest benefit of adhering to Rule 1 is that specifying "next moves" can provide a *quadruple boost in motivation* for the owner of the monkey. First, describing the monkey *clarifies* the "next move," and the more clearly one understands what must be done, the greater the energy and motivation that exist for doing it. (Think about how hesitant you feel about making a move on some vexing problem when you have only a hazy idea of what to do.) Second, specifying the "next move" increases motivation by helping one take the all-important *first step* on a project, which is often the most difficult one to make. After the first step things usually seem easier. Third, specifying "next moves" breaks the project into *bite-size* pieces, and it is much less daunting to think about making a single "next move" on a project—for example, making a phone call—than to worry about all the effort required to complete the entire project. Fourth, describing "next moves" increases motivation by allowing one to *switch his focus* back and forth from goals to "next moves." If the goal—completing the entire project—seems overwhelming, thinking about the "next move"—making a call—is less so, if thinking about all the "next moves" is discouraging, thinking about the satisfaction of achieving the final goal is less so.

Let me relate a couple of instances from my own experience to illustrate the value of the first rule of monkey management. For example, recall the definition of a monkey: *A monkey is the "next move."* This definition does not say anything about ownership. Therefore, it is possible that *one person can own the project and another person can make the "next move."* I often make use of this reality by asking various members of my staff what "next moves" I should make on certain projects of mine. That gives them the "next move" of formulating a recommendation to help me handle my project. This not only synergistically improves the quality of whatever "next move" I make (two heads are better than one even if they only add up to 1.3!), it also develops my people's abilities, and it gives them some insight into the challenges I face. And it helps train my successor (no small matter if I want a promotion).

Another example of using Rule 1 occurs when one of my people and I are discussing a situation and time runs out before we can even finish defining the problem, much less identifying and describing substantive "next moves." Running out of time means the "next move" is to babysit the monkey, i.e., to maintain responsibility for the matter at hand until the discussion is resumed. So I say to the person, "Why don't we talk about this again in a couple of days. In the meantime, you hold on to the problem in case you come up with an idea . . . and I hope you will!"

In the two ensuing days I probably would have done nothing about the monkey, and it is conceivable that my staff member might do *nothing*, too. But if nothing is going to be done, better it be done in her briefcase than mine. Why? Well, for one thing, it's dark inside a briefcase, so the monkey neither knows nor cares whose briefcase it's in. Also, if the monkey is in one of my people's briefcases it is at least conceivable that *something* might get done about it. And even if the *something* amounts to next-to-nothing, that's infinitely more than the nothing I would have done in the same amount of time! Furthermore, even if the *something* is wrong, that's of some value; there are only a finite number of ways to do a thing wrong and she just eliminated one of them!

Here's a final example describing the value of requiring "next moves." Let's say you and a staff member discuss an issue and the dialogue ends with your asking for a recommendation to resolve it. You smile as the two of you part company; *he* has the "next move," which is to formulate the recommendation.

But your pleasure ends with the arrival of his recommendation, a nine-pager, in your in basket. Now *you* have the "next moves": read it, think about it, decide what to do about it, do something about it, and so on. You have the worker role and he the supervisory role.

You can see from this scenario that in monkey business, as in chess and checkers, it pays to think ahead several moves. I have learned to avoid the monkeys just described by having my people *bring* me memos instead of sending them. Why? That way, when the person bearing the memo arrives in my office, I ask him or her to read the memo to me. (Several have indicated they could tell me about the memo in one-third the time it would take to read it, which makes me glad I didn't take the time to read the other two thirds!)

Whether they read it or tell me about it, I have time to think, to watch their facial expressions, and to ask questions. That helps me gain quicker and better understanding than if I had read it myself in isolation, because the memo, being composed of words, is subject to misinterpretation. Also, there is less information *in* the lines of the memo than *between* the lines, and the person who knows the most about what's between the lines is now sitting in front of me to answer any questions I might have.

THERE are countless way to apply Rule 1, but I'm sure you understand the approach by now. So let's move ahead to the next rule, which has to do with assigning ownership of monkeys.

Rule 2 of monkey management states that *the dialogue between boss and staff member must not end until ownership of each monkey is assigned to a person.* This rule is based on several thousand years of human experience that teach us that people take better care of things they own than things they don't. Also, if ownership of the monkey is not specified, nobody assumes personal responsibility for it and it follows that nobody can be held accountable for it.

Thus, the welfare of valuable organizational monkeys demands that they be owned by someone. Therefore, when I and one of my people are discussing a work-related issue, every monkey generated in that discussion must be assigned to one or the other of us before the dialogue ends.

But which monkeys go with whom? I have learned that:

*All
Monkeys
Must Be Handled
At The Lowest
Organizational Level
Consistent With
Their Welfare!*

Keeping the monkeys at the lowest possible level is not, as some view it, buck-passing or abdication of responsibility. On the contrary, there are powerful, legitimate reasons for doing so: (1) my staff has more collective time, energy, and, in many cases, more knowledge for handling monkeys than I do (managers who think they can outperform their entire staff are suffering *delusions of adequacy*); (2) my staff members are closer to their work than I am and are thus in a better position to handle their monkeys, and (3) keeping other people's monkeys out of my office is the only way to preserve some of my own discretionary time.

Consequently, since my "conversion" I have learned to retain *only* the monkeys that *only* I can handle—the rest of them go to my staff. I know there is a limit to how many monkeys my people can handle, so I work hard at making sure they feel free to tell me when they feel they are at their limits (as long as they bring along some recommendations for correcting their problems). But experience has also taught me that my people can often do more than I think they can, and they can sometimes do more than *they* think they can!

If you think as you read this that the practice of pushing monkeys down to the lowest prudent level is easier said than done, I agree. Being a reformed compulsive monkey-picker-upper myself, I am as aware as anyone that there are powerful forces pushing and pulling the monkeys upward.

Hindsight has revealed to me many of the reasons monkeys naturally leap upward. In my case, it was my internal personal needs that, like bananas in a tree, literally lured monkeys upward. The principal reason was that I enjoyed handling my staff's work far more than I enjoyed management. After all, I used to do that kind of work before I became a manager, and I was good at it. (That's why I got promoted!) So doing their work gave me a holiday from the challenges of management (this phenomenon is sometimes referred to as the "executive sandbox" syndrome), and at the same time doing their work provided my staff an opportunity to watch "genius at work"!

Even if I had been aware of all the real reasons I was picking up my staff's monkeys, I don't think I could have admitted them at the time. I now realize that I had concocted an elaborate collection of rationalizations (intellectually respectable, ego-serving reasons for doing things I had no business doing) for picking up monkeys. Have you ever heard any of the following? "If you want it done right you have to do it yourself." "You just can't get good help these days." "This one is just too hot for my staff to handle." "My boss expects me to do this one." "I just want to keep my hand in." "It's easier to do it than to delegate it." "I don't want to ask my people to do anything I'm not willing to do myself."

It is not only internal personal needs that send monkeys to the wrong owners; sometimes organizational policies do it. Some companies are finding, for example, that when the responsibility for product quality is taken away from those who produce the product and given to inspectors, that monkey is on the wrong back. The final product isn't nearly as defect-free. Given these personal and organizational forces, keeping monkeys with their proper owners requires a mixture of both skill and discipline, especially discipline, for without it skill is superfluous.

Great discipline is needed to overcome the following *apparent* paradox in management: Sometimes when you insist on the very best in your people's work, you may encounter resistance because doing the very best often requires hard work. On the other hand, if you permit your people to be less than their best, they sometimes don't actively resist. So it sometimes *seems* that they would rather do less than their best.

The dynamics of that apparent paradox work against the practice of keeping monkeys with their proper owners because it is sometimes easier to pick up the monkeys than to deal with the problems of keeping them on the backs of their rightful owners. But, beware . . . the paradox is only apparent, not real, as the great managers and leaders of history have taught us.

The leaders we remember most appreciatively are those who knew that in the long run other people, despite their apparent resistance, will respect you—even love you—if you help bring out the best in them.

To strengthen your resolve in this regard, think back to your school days. Which teachers do you remember most fondly? The ones I remember best were a few taskmasters who pushed me to the limit to do my best. And did I ever resist the pressure! At times I thought I hated them. (I think I sometimes prayed for their death!) But I did my best for them because deep down I knew they had my best interests at heart. Now I appreciate them above all the others, some of whom I don't even remember. In fact, I have found myself at times resenting those people who let me waste part of my life even though it was my own fault.

I demand excellence from myself and I expect no less from my staff. I still get some resistance when I challenge them to their limits. If they resist, I listen to them, but I keep in mind the example of my teachers and some of the other great managers I have known and heard about. When they resist, I recall the story of the farmer who, when asked by his neighbor why he was working his sons so hard just to grow corn, replied, "I'm not just growing corn. I'm growing sons!"

Remember:

*The Only Way
To Develop
Responsibility In People
Is To Give Them
Responsibility*

*

Now that you have some ideas about the *discipline* required to keep monkeys with their proper owners, I want to tell you about a few of my experiences that will help you improve your *skill* in applying the second rule of monkey management.

Before I learned these things, one of my people, Gordon, was a veritable monkey factory! Every time I saw him—in hallways, cafeteria lines, elevators, parking lots—his first words to me were "We've got a problem." Almost invariably I wound up with the monkey, and usually it was *his* monkey.

Since then, I have learned to avoid the care and feeding of Gordon's monkeys by using an *anti-straddle reflex* that is instantly provoked by the word "we." When I hear the phrase "We've got a problem" I visualize a straddling monkey with one leg on my back and the other on Gordon's back. Then I remember the dangers of this posture . . . the monkey might get a hernia, and I might get somebody else's monkey! That mental picture triggers an instantaneous and automatic response in my central nervous system.

I say to Gordon, "*We* do not have a problem, and *we* will never again have one. I'm sure there is a problem, but it is not ours, it is either yours or mine. The first item on the agenda is to neaten up the pronouns and find out whose problem this is. If it turns out to be my problem, I hope you will help me with it. If it turns out to be your problem, I will help you with it subject to the following condition: at no time while I'm helping you with your problem will your problem become my problem, because the minute your problem becomes my problem, you will no longer have a problem and I can't help a person who does not have a problem!"

By the time I finish my little speech the person wonders why he even brought it up. He figures he would be better off solving the problem himself than listening to me. But after the shock subsides we discuss the problem. Then we identify "next moves." I assign as many as possible to him and retain only those that are rightfully mine.

This process has taught Gordon, my "monkey factory," that the monkey can be owned by only one person, and that *he* owns it until the facts prove otherwise, and that the burden of proof is on him. For me to assume the burden of proof would be to pick up a monkey I should not have. That way the monkey never begins the straddle; it stays on Gordon's back until rightful ownership has been ascertained.

If Gordon convinces me it's my monkey, I calmly and deliberately reach over and take it; if it turns out to be his monkey, I don't have to delegate it because I don't have it—he still has it! Nowadays the phrase "We've got a problem" is seldom heard around my department.

In another instance, sheer paralysis on my part taught me a valuable lesson about keeping monkeys with their proper owners. It began when one of my people, Leesa, said to me, "Boss, *I've* got a problem." I replied, "A problem? Be positive. There's no such thing as problems. Just opportunities!" She replied, "In that case, I've got an insurmountable opportunity." After a good laugh, I asked her, "What's the problem?"

Leesa described her problem, but she offered no solutions. She stood there silently; I suppose she was waiting for me to tell her what to do. At that time I was so new at monkey management I didn't know what to say or do, so I stood there, stone silent, trying to figure out what to do next. The silence grew longer. I was uncomfortable. I don't know what Leesa was thinking, but finally she broke the silence by blurting out, "Why don't I think this thing over a little longer. I'm sure I can come up with something."

The discomfort of the silence caused Leesa to identify the monkey, assume and acknowledge ownership of it, and beat a hasty retreat! Although I learned that technique by accident, I have used it to good effect on other occasions. I have also learned other variations of it; in addition to silence, the discomfort that stimulates a person to snatch the monkey and run can be caused by a full bladder after several cups of coffee, or by a meeting that goes on past quitting time.

I am reminded of the story I once read about how a famous person handled the problem of upward-leaping monkeys in the form of incomplete work from one of his people. This staff member had not responded to any of the normal remedies, so the manager decided to try something drastic. The very next time he received an incomplete proposal from this person, he returned it with a note saying, "You're better than this!" The subordinate improved and resubmitted the proposal only to get it back the second time with another note: "Is this the very best you can do on this?" Again the person improved the proposal. This time he personally delivered it to his boss and said, "This is absolutely the best I can do on this matter," whereupon his boss replied, "Good. Now I'll read it."

78 / Rule 3 *Insurance Policies*

WELL, that's it for Rule 2, assigning ownership of monkeys. Now that they are on the proper backs, let's get the little buggers insured before we send them out to face the dangers of the organizational jungle.

Rule 3 of monkey management states that *the dialogue between boss and staff member shall not end until all monkeys have been insured.* This rule provides a systematic way to balance your staff's need for freedom in handling their monkeys with, simultaneously, your responsibility for the outcome.

Giving your people authority and freedom benefits both you and them. The benefit to you is discretionary time—the more freedom they have, the less of your time and energy is required to supervise them. At the same time, freedom allows your people to enjoy the many benefits of self-management (more satisfaction, more energy, higher morale, and the like).

But every benefit has its costs. The cost of giving your people more freedom is the increased risk that freedom entails. When people have freedom, they will make mistakes. Monkey insurance is designed to make sure they make *only affordable mistakes*! That is why all monkeys must be insured by one of the following policies:

MONKEY INSURANCE POLICIES

1. RECOMMEND, THEN ACT
2. ACT, THEN ADVISE

Level 1, *Recommend, Then Act*, provides insurance in situations where I feel there is a reasonable risk that one of my people might make an *un*affordable mistake if left to his or her own devices. In such cases, where I think my staff's actions might "burn the building down," I want a chance to blow out the match beforehand, that is, I want a chance to veto their proposed actions. Such anxieties are usually connected with matters so important that if they were botched, I could not fire the botcher for incompetence because I myself would no longer have the authority. On these matters I require my people to formulate recommendations that I must approve *before* they can proceed any further. This provides protection, but at the cost of more of my time and some of my people's freedom.

Level 2 insurance, *Act, Then Advise*, is for monkeys I'm pretty sure my people can handle successfully on their own. They are free to resolve these matters and inform me afterward at whatever time they think is appropriate. This gives them a lot of operating room and saves me a lot of supervisory time. The risk is that if they take an action that is going to burn the building down I won't learn about it until afterward, when it is too late to do anything but hose down the ashes.

Who selects the insurance policy for a given situation? Although I, as manager, must ultimately *approve* all selections, either party might *make* the selection depending on the circumstances. Sometimes I make the selection, especially when I require the protection afforded by Level 1. My people sometimes complain a little when I choose Level 1 because it limits their freedom, but it would be abdicating my responsibility as a manager for me to allow them to operate on their own with Level 2 insurance when there is a significant risk of an unaffordable mistake.

Of course, it is neither possible nor desirable for me to tell my people in advance which policy to use on each and every thing they do. So, on most endeavors they assume the responsibility—and the risk!—of selecting the policy themselves (with the understanding that their selections must ultimately satisfy me). They elect to use Level 2 only when, in their judgment, they believe that it will be acceptable to me if they go ahead and handle the situation in their own manner and inform me later. Otherwise, they give me their recommendations in advance and then proceed with whatever actions we agree to in the dialogue (Level 1). If I am not satisfied with the policy they are using, I have the prerogative to change it. My aim is to:

*

*Practice
Hands-Off Management
As Much As
Possible
And
Hands-On Management
As Much As
Necessary*

*

Rule 3 *Insurance Policies* / 83

I do this by *encouraging* my people to utilize Level 2 insurance as much as possible and *requiring* them to use Level 1 insurance as much as necessary.

Insuring monkeys is a dynamic process. A person will do some parts of his work with Level 1 authority and other parts with Level 2 authority. What is done with one level of insurance today might later require another level if circumstances change. In the following examples you will see the policies changing, sometimes on the discretion of my people and sometimes on my discretion.

The first example is the case of one of my former employees, Alex, who exercised more freedom than my anxieties would tolerate. He preferred to handle all his monkeys on a Level 2 basis and inform me only occasionally of what he was doing, seemingly immune to my requests to keep me better informed.

One day there was a huge problem with one of his projects. My boss found out about it before I did and expressed her displeasure to me in unmistakable terms. I went straight to Alex's office and did the same thing to him. I told him about how his not keeping me informed led to the unpleasant surprise I had just endured in my boss's office. I was furious. "All I'm asking is that you keep me informed, but you never do. But we'll fix that! From now on, don't do anything on this project until you check with me first."

Perhaps I overreacted, but nevertheless, Alex was the case of someone whose actions were such that my anxieties could not tolerate them at the time. In order to get my anxieties down to a level that allowed me to sleep at night, I had to move him back from Level 2 authority to Level 1. He complied, but, as you might suspect, he eased himself back into Level 2 after I calmed down and the project stabilized.

That was a case where someone exercised too much freedom; the next example has to do with an occasion where I *gave* one of my people too much freedom. Maria was somewhat anxious about a certain project and wouldn't make any substantial moves on it without checking with me first. She was using Level 1 insurance to get my fingerprints on everything she did. I was sure she could handle this project without checking with me so often, so I assured her of my confidence and asked her to resolve the matter on her own and let me know what she had done.

After Maria left my office I got a little concerned that if she was so anxious about the project, perhaps I should be, too. I began wondering if I had overlooked something important. I called her back and asked what was the worst thing that could go wrong with this project and what were the odds it would go wrong? Her answer almost gave me a heart attack! My knees turned to water. I was sweating. My hands were trembling.

I was petrified! Two years earlier, my fears would have caused me to yank that monkey off Maria's back, clutch it to my chest, and handle it myself. This time, however, I increased my protection by merely reinsuring it from Level 2 to Level 1. I told Maria, "On second thought, please let me know your plans before you take any further action on this matter." Then I slumped back into my chair, exhausted but relieved that I had caught the situation in time.

Later, as the project settled down and both Maria and I grew more comfortable with it and with each other, on her own discretion she moved to Level 2 authority on most aspects of it.

As it turned out, though, that project later became so important my boss, Alice, began keeping closer tabs on it. One day she called to ask how it was going and I told her I was letting Maria handle most of it on her own (Level 2) because she had earned the right to do so and because I wanted to let her grow and shine. My boss told me that because of the customer involved, she wanted me to handle the matter personally. When I tried to dissuade her she told me something that really summed up the philosophy of balancing people's desire for freedom with the organization's need for protection: "I appreciate what you're doing," she said, "but this project is too risky for that. There will be other opportunities for developing your people." She told me to remember . . .

*

*Never
Let The Company
Go Down The Drain
Simply
For The Sake Of
Practicing
Good Management*

*

Rule 4 *Feeding and Checkups*

THE output of any organization is the sum of a myriad of "next moves," which means that the success of a company is a function of the health of its monkeys. Because monkey health is so vital, monkeys *must* have periodic checkups to maintain their well-being. That is the reason for Rule 4 of monkey management, which states that *the dialogue between boss and staff member shall not end until the monkey has a checkup appointment.*

Since monkeys sometimes develop unexpected problems, checkups are crucial. Wise people, even if they are healthy, schedule regular medical checkups in order to detect problems and correct them. Likewise with monkeys. If the checkup reveals problems, a treatment is devised. However, if the checkup shows the monkey to be in good health, good news is in order for its owner. So the purpose of monkey checkups is twofold: one, to catch people doing something right and praise them for it, and two, to spot problems and take corrective action before the problems become crises. The process of discovering and correcting problems tends to (1) lower the boss's anxieties, and (2) develop people's competence through coaching—which increases the boss's confidence in their competence and further decreases his or her anxieties, and (3) the coaching increases the odds that the boss will eventually be able to delegate to that person.

That is why no monkey leaves my office on the back of one of my people until the date for its checkup has been set. I prefer to minimize the number of *scheduled* checkups, so I like to schedule appointments as far in the future as would be advisable *if* the monkey were to receive no checkups in the interim. However, I have an understanding with my people that if anything arises in the meantime that makes either them or me nervous about the health of a monkey, either of us may take the initiative to move up the monkey's checkup appointment to an earlier time.

Here is an example of a monkey malady and of why rescheduled checkups are occasionally necessary. Sometimes when I am walking around keeping myself informed and letting my people know I am interested in them and what they are doing, I might notice a monkey that looks sick (it is suffering either malnutrition from lack of attention, or some illness from improper treatment). The monkey's problem is seldom the result of laziness, carelessness, malice, or anything like that; it is usually sick because my people, like all busy people, have to set priorities, and when they do, the monkeys at the bottom of the list sometimes suffer. And usually the reason they have not already told me about the monkey is because most of my people would rather solve their own problems than bring them to me . . . *which can be a problem in itself!*

Rule 4 *Feeding and Checkups* / 89

For example, Erik, a member of my staff, is an extremely competent, diligent person who is so highly self-reliant that he will do his best to nurse an ailing monkey back to health before getting me involved. Such self-reliance is commendable unless taken to the extreme. Erik takes it to the extreme. He would not even inform me that the monkey had a tummy ache (must less ask for my help) until the poor creature was nearly beyond saving. Then my office would become an emergency room, where I would have to drop everything else I was doing in order to deal with the crisis. In a sense, a routine appendectomy became a ruptured appendix with massive infection simply because I had not been informed a little earlier.

Before I learned better I would show my displeasure at such developments by giving Erik a lecture on the importance of monkey health, and ranting and raving because he had allowed the situation to degenerate. I have since learned two much more constructive ways to head off most crises and show my concern for monkeys.

One is developing an understanding between my people and me that they will treat their sick monkeys' maladies as best they can, but if the condition persists or worsens and does not respond to treatment, the monkey will be brought to my office for a checkup in time for me to get involved *before* its vital signs have disappeared.

In other words, if someone like Erik can't heal the monkey, and if there is a chance the little dear might not survive until the next scheduled checkup, it is Erik's responsibility to initiate an interim, precautionary checkup.

On the other hand, if I discover the malady, I deal with it by simply moving the next checkup appointment to a time warranted by the condition of the monkey. For example, if the sick monkey had been previously scheduled for a checkup in my office three weeks hence, I change that time to twenty-four hours hence. That sends a powerful message about my concern for the monkey.

An interesting example of this takes place when a monkey is in jeopardy due to inattention by its owner, that is, *something* should have been done about it but because *nothing* has been done, the project is in trouble. In that case, I move up the checkup appointment appropriately. Sometimes the person will request more time before the new checkup in order to get something done on the monkey. The reasoning, as some have explained, is that since nothing has been done, there is nothing to discuss during the checkup. But there is something very important to discuss—the fact that nothing has been done and the implications of that fact!

Rule 4 *Feeding and Checkups* / 91

Moreover, if I give people more time because they have done nothing, I will reward their doing nothing, and what I reward I will get more of! In other words, if I allow the rendering of accountability to be delayed until whenever my people might happen to be ready, the monkey could starve or get sicker in the meantime.

So my response is that we will conduct the checkup anyway and discuss the "nothing" that has been done. This leaves the person facing two unpleasant courses of action: one, continue doing *nothing* and come into my office the next day and make a "lack of progress" report, or, two, do *something* and bring me a progress report. The result is predictable: my staff member digs in and progress on the monkey is miraculously made. A progress report made under conditions just described might be superficial the first time, but think about what the person learns with respect to handling future occasions. Anyway, *my* moving up a monkey's checkup appointment because *I* discovered it was starving to death is, in itself, a monkey I should never have in the first place.

The examples just described had to do with sick monkeys. An opposite problem occurs when the monkey is quite healthy and vigorous but is not the kind of monkey I envisioned when it was born. For example, not too long ago I was discussing a project with Ben, one of my people. We discussed the general aspects of the design, budget, and timing. I was sure we had achieved a good understanding about *what* was to be done so I largely left it up to him as to *how* to do it.

92 / Rule 4 *Feeding and Checkups*

But the next time I checked on the matter, the design had gone off in a whole new direction and the potential cost of the project had gone through the roof, all of which was totally unacceptable to me. There can be many causes of such a problem: misunderstanding, conditions that change along the way, Ben's belief that his new design is better than what we agreed on, and so on. Periodic checkups tend to highlight the existence of such problems and limit their costs by allowing a manager to detect the problem and see to it that it is corrected.

Now a final note about checkup appointments. I used to be extremely reluctant to perform checkups on monkeys because I did not differentiate between checking up on monkeys and checking up on people. I thought checkups were the equivalent of snooping on people and assuming they would not do good work unless prodded by me. Since then, however, I have come to understand that checkups focus more on the monkeys' condition than on the people themselves, so checkups give me the opportunity to "catch people doing something right," detect and correct problems with monkeys, coach my people, reduce my anxiety level, and the like. After that, my people take care of their performance themselves (this is why managing monkeys properly means you don't have to manage people so much).

Because monkey checkups are so vital, they must be treated with great respect by both bosses and staff. And if the boss treats them as important, the staff will tend to do so as well. Therefore, I do anything I can to emphasize to my people the importance of checkup appointments. For example, when we schedule a checkup appointment, I make a point of writing it on my calender; *writing* the date gives the appointment more legitimacy and value than merely stating it. And if I am going to be late for an appointment, I make every effort to let my people know in advance. That not only illustrates the importance I attach to checkups, it also shows that I value punctuality as well.

Doing those things shows what I stand for and, by implication, *what I won't stand for.* People need to know both. So, for example, if one of my people is late or absent for an appointment and could have informed me in advance but didn't, I make things a little unpleasant. I deliver a little speech about how the next time he or she is unable to keep an appointment a call from the hospital will be cheerfully accepted. I rarely have to make this speech with any of my people anymore.

A SUMMARY OF ONCKEN'S FOUR RULES OF MONKEY MANAGEMENT

Rule 1. *Describe the Monkey:* The dialogue must not end until appropriate "next moves" have been identified and specified.

Rule 2. *Assign the Monkey:* All monkeys shall be owned and handled at the lowest organizational level consistent with their welfare.

Rule 3. *Insure the Monkey:* Every monkey leaving your presence on the back of one of your people must be covered by one of two insurance policies:
   1. Recommend, Then Act
   2. Act, Then Advise

Rule 4. *Check on the Monkey:* Proper follow-up means healthier monkeys. Every monkey should have a checkup appointment.

So far, we have progressed from the disaster of my *working* all my people's monkeys to the point where I have *assigned* the monkeys to my staff. And you have learned how I applied the four rules of monkey management.

Let me now tell you about my progression to the ultimate degree of management, *delegation*, where my people are achieving more and more with less and less involvement from me. Assigning my staff's monkeys to them is miles ahead of working their monkeys myself, and delegation is light-years ahead of assigning. The best way to understand delegation (and how to achieve it) is to understand how it differs from assigning. Although many people use the words interchangeably, the words are, to quote Mark Twain, "as different as lightning from a lightning bug." That critical difference is one of the most valuable insights I gained from the "Managing Management Time" seminar:

*

*Assigning
Involves
A
Single
Monkey;
Delegation
Involves
A Family
Of Monkeys*

*

When I assigned a monkey to be handled by a member of my staff, I did most of the work of assigning. I described the monkey, I designated an owner for it, I insured it, and I scheduled and performed checkups on it. In other words, I assigned the monkeys, my people worked them.

We have since moved ahead to *delegation* where my staff are not only *working* their monkeys as before, they are also *assigning* them. Everything that was formerly done by them and me together, they are now doing on their own. In addition to working the monkeys, my people also identify them, insure them, assume ownership of them, and perform their own checkups on the monkeys. They themselves are applying Oncken's Rules of Monkey Management to their monkeys!

To put it differently, my people are now managing whole families of monkeys (projects) on their own for extended periods of time with minimal involvement from me. My involvement is limited to checking on the overall project from time to time, which means I don't have to get involved with the scores of individual monkeys that constitute the project, and a project checkup requires far less time than checking on each of the monkeys.

Between checkups my people are fully responsible for their projects (unless we encounter a problem that requires my intervention). As such, they are practicing *self-management,* which we all like a lot better than the high degree of *boss-management* they experienced when I was assigning monkeys to them.

In order to fully appreciate why delegation is the ultimate degree of professional management, let's recall a famous old definition of management: *Management is getting things done through others.* By that definition, the ultimate measure of management is *results*—the staff's output resulting from a manager's input. Other things being equal, the greater the ratio of output-to-input, the more effective the manager is.

Observe how the output-to-input ratio increased as I and my staff advanced from *doing* to *assigning* and then from *assigning* to *delegating.* When I was doing all the work myself, my output was equal to my input—one hour of input produced one hour of output. My department's output was sadly limited to the output of just one person . . . me!

Next, after some guidance from the One Minute Manager and learning from the seminar, I began assigning the monkeys to my people. My output-to-input ratio increased because every hour I spent assigning monkeys resulted in several hours of work produced by my staff. I welcomed that increase, but the ratio was still far too small because my input was still so large. (I was spending a lot of time on each individual monkey.) My department's output was still constrained by the large amount of time my people spent dealing with *me* and by the limited number of monkeys I had time to assign.

However, now that we have achieved the state of affairs called delegation, my output-to-input ratio has soared to many times what it was previously. My *input* is now dramatically lower—instead of doing all the work entailed in assigning scores of individual monkeys, I merely have to check on the condition of the whole project occasionally. And my department's *output* has now expanded enormously for two reasons: one, my people don't have to spend as much time with me as before, and two, they have more energy and motivation and morale for handling monkeys that are self-imposed than if the same monkeys were boss-imposed.

MOREOVER, reaching the state of delegation on one project frees up some time for me to pursue delegation on other projects. As I achieve delegation on more and more projects, more and more discretionary time is released to spend with my boss, peers, customers, and—myself.

Once delegation is reached, staying there is easy compared with the job of getting there. The state of "delegation" is analogous to an airplane at cruise altitude on automatic pilot where the pilot only monitors the flight and intervenes occasionally, if at all. But those interventions are minuscule in comparison with the energy and work the pilot expends in getting the plane away from the gate, down the runway, off the ground, and up to cruising altitude.

How does one attain this delightful state of delegation? The One Minute Manager explained that in its broadest sense, "coaching" is the term commonly used to signify the things managers do with their people to get projects up to "cruise altitude," where they can and will be handled mostly by staff members with minimal intervention by the manager. Remember:

*

*The
Purpose Of
Coaching
Is
To Get Into
Position
To
Delegate!*

*

What exactly has to happen before one is in position to delegate? Managers must not, indeed cannot, delegate until they are reasonably confident that (1) the project is on the right track, and (2) their people can successfully handle the project on their own. Managers who give their people full project responsibility and authority without such confidence are not delegating—they are abdicating responsibility.

Obviously, some projects can be delegated at the outset because it is sufficiently clear to the manager in the beginning how they should be handled and that staff members can successfully handle them.

However, most endeavors with the dimensions and complexities of a project cannot be delegated at the outset because often, in the beginning of a project, neither the manager nor his or her staff member has sufficient understanding of the problems, goals, options, timing, and ramifications to know even how to proceed, much less know whether that person can handle the project successfully. Thus, most projects require a period of coaching before the boss has sufficient confidence to enable him or her to delegate responsibly.

Obviously staff members *must* play a large role in building their boss's confidence to the point where the boss can delegate. In the first place, managers cannot delegate until their people have somehow demonstrated that they can handle the project.

Moreover, since people usually know more about their jobs than their bosses know, in many cases they should be persuading their bosses how the project should be handled. *This makes people just as responsible for coaching and delegation as their bosses are!*

The best way I know to explain the process of coaching is to describe a recent experience with one of my people, Gordon. As you will recall, he was my "monkey factory." This experience is one of my proudest accomplishments as a manager because I think it shows how much I and my people have improved in the past two years. First I will briefly describe what happened; then we can analyze it.

Some time ago it became apparent to me that one of our products might be having some technical problems in some of our customer locations. Before I got around to taking any action on the matter, Gordon, who was in charge of the product, stopped by my office one day and updated me on the situation. Only then did I realize that this had the potential of becoming a very costly and embarrassing problem. He had already prepared his recommendation for dealing with the problem so we made a date to meet the next day to discuss it.

Gordon conducted the meeting. His proposed solution consisted of a one-page synopsis followed by eighteen pages of supporting information in case it was needed. He read and then we discussed his synopsis, which contained a clear, brief description of the situation, three possible options for resolving it, the pros and cons of each option, and the option he recommended we adopt. As it turned out, no one was sure if the source of the problem was our company's product or the other products connected with it. So Gordon's solution included first a study to identify the nature and scope of the problem, and then corrective measures later if necessary to fix the problem.

It was soon obvious that Gordon had covered every detail of the technical part of the situation. (I was thankful he did, because my technical skills have necessarily diminished since I've been a manager.) He had determined what should be done, when, by whom, and how much it would cost. He specified all the resources he would need—budget, authority, and manpower—and the help he would need from me in arranging for them. His technical preparations left nothing to be desired.

However, there was a snag. Gordon had not fully considered how his proposed solution might be received by our sales people, the customers, and our higher management people. I explained that I was especially concerned about the reactions of two of our vice-presidents whose support would be critical to this endeavor, and I asked him what he thought we should do.

Gordon convinced me he could persuade the vice-presidents to support the project, so I asked him to meet with them to inform them of his plans and solicit their advice, and then report back to me before moving ahead on the project. When we met again he reported that despite his best efforts, one of the VPs still had serious reservations. He recommended that I speak to the VP. "Okay," I told Gordon, "I will do that, but you're going with me to watch what I do and help me as much as possible."

Two meetings with the VP and some minor changes to our plans resolved the problem and eliminated the last obstacle to my willingness to delegate the remainder of the project to Gordon, which I did. Then we made a date for a month afterward to go over the results of his study before we took any further steps. At that point, he took control of the project for a month, during which he handled dozens and dozens of monkeys on his own.

Now, let's analyze that scenario and look at the many things that helped me get into position to delegate—and let's pay special attention to *who* did those things!

1. *I cannot delegate until my anxieties allow it.* Gordon helped lower my anxieties by convincing me he could handle *most* aspects of the situation on his own. His thorough preparation and his skillful presentation plus his past record of success on similar projects were the main convincers. However, some residual anxieties caused me to retain control for a time. I maintained control by giving Gordon assignments (monkeys) which were insured at Level 1 (Recommend, Then Act). On assignments he could not handle alone, I worked the monkey *with* him—not *for* him—so I could do some teaching in the process.

2. *I can delegate only if I am reasonably sure my people know what is to be done.* But before they can know what to do, someone has to figure out what to do. If I figure it out, then I must tell them what to do (which is autocratic management). So Gordon figured out what to do himself, and then persuaded me he was right. That saved me a lot of time, and he was much more committed to his own ideas than any I might think up.

3. *It would be foolish to delegate to someone without reasonable assurance that he or she can get sufficient resources—time, information, money, people, assistance, and authority—to do the work.* But who could know better than Gordon what resources he needed? That's why *he* took the initiative to determine what these resources were. Moreover, on his own Gordon arranged for as many of the resources as possible, asking for my help in arranging only those things he could not get for himself.

4. *I cannot turn control of any project over to anyone until I am confident that the cost and timing and quantity and quality of the project will be acceptable.* To leave those items open-ended would be abdicating my responsibility as a manager. But in order to *agree* on standards of performance, we must first *have* some, which means that someone must produce them. The person who should produce them is the person who is in the best position to know what the standards should be. Gordon was, he did, and he convinced me to approve them.

5. It is clear that the more committed my people are to their projects the greater the odds of their projects' success. Other things being equal, *the more commitment my people show, the more comfortable I will be in delegating to them.* Gordon took care of his own commitment. The time and effort he *invested* in his proposal increased his commitment. The fact that it was *his* proposal increased his commitment, as did his personal pride in doing a job well. Gordon's implicit promise to me to do the work sealed his commitment. Because his commitment was internally generated, I did not have to resort to requests or contracts or coercion to gain his commitment.

This is not an exhaustive list of things that have to happen before delegation can occur, but it illustrates the process. Regarding Gordon, I'm sure you noticed that I maintained control of the project until I was confident I could delegate control to him. But *he* initiated and carried out most of the "next moves" that got us to the point of delegation. That was as it should be. Since the purpose of coaching is to get my people to the point where they can succeed on their own, it would defeat the purpose if I were to do anything, even in the coaching process, that they could do themselves.

The coaching process usually consists of staff members carrying out a series of assignments while managers control and direct the process until they are confident their people can assume control for an extended period on their own. As the assignments are carried out, both the manager and his or her people gain time and information they can use to sharpen their thinking about where the project should be heading. As they both become more confident that the project is on the right track and as the boss's confidence in the person's competence grows, the boss gradually delegates more and more project responsibility. The assignments should be boss-initiated *only to the extent the staff member cannot initiate them*. Usually, the first assignments are for the subordinate to develop and propose a "game plan." If necessary, the boss redirects the plan until it is acceptable to him or her. Then, if the parties are still not in position to delegate, the next assignments are for the subordinate to make some "next moves" on the project itself with the boss guiding and controlling the process until delegation can occur. You can see from this that, usually, delegation is not just an act; it is usually a state of affairs that exists only after sufficient coaching enables the boss to delegate responsibly.

Of course, not all coaching experiences are as easy as the one just described. But they tend to get easier after managers and their people go through the process a few times because everyone learns to anticipate and complement the other, much like a passer and receiver on a football team. After sufficient practice a quarterback can throw the ball to a spot on the field before the receiver ever turns toward that spot because he knows exactly where the receiver will be going and exactly when he will arrive. Furthermore, each can make the other a better player. With a great catch the receiver can make a poor pass successful, and with a great pass the thrower can make the receiver successful. Likewise with managers and their people. Once they learn to work together they can achieve the point where people conceive and implement most of their work, while the boss merely ratifies what is being done.

A lot has happened since the One Minute Manager told me about Oncken's monkey management. When I think how much my life has changed, I sometimes recall the story of the man who, when asked how long he had been working for his company, replied, "Ever since they threatened to fire me!"

Like him, I was shocked into action. The conversion wasn't always easy. I encountered a good deal of resistance and I made some mistakes. But I finally got the responsibility where it should be, and things have never been the same since, and they never will be the same again!

As I applied the concepts I've learned, my people became more self-managed than ever before. That made them feel better and perform better. They became more self-reliant, which gave me more time to manage other relationships that were vital to my department's success.

Let me pause here for a moment or two and reflect on those other relationships and one last important lesson I got from the Oncken "Managing Management Time" seminar. While monkey management is key to controlling what Oncken called "subordinate-imposed" time (where a boss is handling monkeys that his or her people should be caring for and feeding), success in management requires that we constantly strike a proper balance among three categories of time:

THREE KINDS OF ORGANIZATIONAL TIME:

BOSS-IMPOSED TIME

SYSTEM-IMPOSED TIME

SELF-IMPOSED TIME

BOSS-*imposed time* is time you and I spend doing things we would not be doing if we did not have bosses. No one has to have a boss; one can retire, go on welfare, win the lottery, or become an entrepreneur, and thereby avoid having one. But having a boss *requires* some of our time because of the Golden Rule of Management: THOSE WHO HAVE THE GOLD MAKE THE RULES!

Because bosses have Golden Rule clout, we intuitively understand that it's to our advantage that they be satisfied with our work. Keeping bosses satisfied takes time, but dealing with dissatisfied ones takes even more time.

For example, back in the days when I was so busy with my staff's monkeys, one of my many mistakes was not taking time to keep my boss well-enough informed about what was going on. As a result, she got an embarrassing surprise one day when her boss uncovered a big problem I should have warned her about in advance.

Her reaction was to institute a whole new set of reports from me to her. That took more of my time than if I had kept her informed in the first place.

How do I keep my boss satisfied with my work? Here is the best expression on how to do it I've ever heard. Always do what your boss wants. If you don't like what your boss wants, *change what your boss wants*, but always do what your boss wants.

This is not to say that we should always agree with our bosses. On the contrary:

*

*If
You Always
Agree
With
Your Boss,
One
Of You
Is Not
Necessary*

*

But it is to your advantage to satisfy your boss. So if you disagree with what your boss wants, treat your boss the same way you want your people to treat you when they disagree with something you want. We call it *loyal opposition*. That's when you try to convince your boss to accept some better alternative; but failing that, always wholeheartedly do what he or she wants.

One of the most important lessons of my career is that good work alone, no matter how much it satisfies *you*, might not be enough to satisfy your boss. Satisfying your boss takes time, sometimes over and above the time it takes to do the good work. I realize it takes time to keep *my* boss informed, to protect her from embarrassing surprises, to anticipate how she wants things handled, to build a record of success so she feels more comfortable giving me more autonomy, and so on.

We neglect doing these things at our peril. Believe me, I know from experience that failing to invest sufficient time to satisfy my boss will soon result in more and more boss-imposed time, which, of course, means less and less time available to spend with my peers or associates and staff and on the things I would like to do.

SYSTEM-*imposed time* is time we spend on the administrative and related demands from people (peers/associates) other than our bosses and our own staffs, demands that are part of every organization. This is the time spent as just one of a seemingly countless number of pulleys on an endless administrative conveyor belt crisscrossing the organizational chart, dropping things off and picking things up. For you, the drop-off point is your "in basket" and the pick-up point is your "out basket." System-imposed time includes administrative forms to be completed, meetings you have to attend, and phone calls you must handle.

For example, if your secretary elopes, that creates in your department what is called in Personnel language "an unfilled vacancy." (When they fill it they call it a "filled vacancy.") If you ask them to hire another secretary for you, they will ask you to fill out a form, write a job description, and so on. The time you spend dealing with these matters is system-imposed time. Some people call it red tape, some call it administrivia, some call it bureaucracy.

Administrative red tape exists in virtually all organizations because staff departments that employ people to support everyone in line management are typically overworked and understaffed.

A support person once explained to me why things are this way: "There is no limit to how much can be asked of us, but there is definitely a limit to how much we can do!" Therefore, support people can't possibly do everything that is requested of them. So, in order to bring order out of chaos and to make their own lives a little easier, they develop wondrous varieties of forms, policies, procedures, and manuals.

The red tape takes time, so a lot of people complain about it. But ignoring the system's requirements is risky. Oncken told a wonderful story about a manager whose chair had collapsed and who wanted it replaced. Because he was busy he had not taken the time to get to know anyone in Purchasing, nor did he take the time to go see them face to face to request a new chair. Instead, he made his request over the phone.

He was under a lot of pressure at the time and was annoyed because of the broken chair so he was somewhat curt to the person in Purchasing. "We'll have to have that request in writing. And on the proper form" was the equally curt reply. He didn't have the proper form so he walked over to Purchasing and, trying to keep his cool but obviously annoyed, filled out the form right there and shoved it across the counter.

Ten days later (when he was expecting his new chair) that request form showed up in his in basket with a note stapled to it that said, "Sorry. We cannot process this request because you have the wrong authorization number in Box 9." He was livid. He called Purchasing and chewed them out. When he finally calmed down he asked them, "What is the right number?" With an audible chuckle the clerk gave him an answer that was quick and to the point: "Let's get something straight. Our job is to spot the wrong numbers and your job is to fill in the right ones." The manager repaired the old chair himself.

We can't manage without the support of these people, and we need them more than they need us. So, in order to survive within the organization, we have to conform to the red-tape requirements of the system. If we give their requirements short shrift in order to spend our time elsewhere, they can penalize us in ways that require even more system-imposed time.

Self-Imposed Time

THE third kind of time we must manage successfully is *self-imposed time*, which is time spent doing the things *we* decide to do, not things done strictly in response to the initiatives of our bosses, peers, and the people who report to us. You can't be a self-starter without self-imposed time.

Self-imposed time is the most important of the three types of time because that's the only time in which we have discretion to express our own individuality within an organization. In boss-imposed time the boss's requirements take precedence over our own individuality. In system-imposed time the need to conform takes precedence. Therefore, it is only with self-imposed time that we make our own unique contribution to an organization.

Self-imposed time, like cholesterol, comes in two varieties, good and bad: discretionary and subordinate-imposed. Subordinate-imposed time, as we have explained, is time spent working on your staff's monkeys. (It is obviously self-imposed because we can elect whether to pick up the monkeys or not.)

DISCRETIONARY time is time in which we do the things that make our work truly rewarding over and above financial compensation—things such as creating, innovating, leading, planning, and organizing. And these activities are needed in organizations for growth and progress and to remain viable and competitive. Discretionary time is thus vital to individuals and to the organization.

Although discretionary time is the most vital time of all, it is, unfortunately, the first to disappear when the pressure is on, as I learned so well in the school of hard knocks.

Why? The reason has to do with the incentive system. You see, if we don't comply with our bosses' wishes we will be guilty of *insubordination*. If we don't conform to the system's requirements we will be guilty of *noncooperation*. If we don't do what we promised for our staff, that is, work off their monkeys, we will be guilty of *procrastination*. We are very reluctant to be guilty of such organizational sins because:

*

*Swift And Obvious
Penalties
Pursue Those
Who Treat Other People's
Requirements In A
Lighthearted,
Cavalier Fashion!*

*

But, what is the penalty for neglecting the most important kind of time of all: discretionary time? For instance, what is the penalty for neglecting to do the things I dream up in my discretionary time (especially if no one else knows about them)? There is no penalty, at least in the short term, because nobody can accuse me of not doing what they never knew I intended to do in the first place.

So discretionary activities (which carry no immediate penalties) compete for my time with activities which, if neglected, make me guilty of either insubordination, noncooperation, or procrastination. Guess which ones take precedence!

While neglecting discretionary time might be safe in the short run, in the long run the penalties are severe both to the organization and to myself. The long-term penalty to the organization is that it cannot survive, much less progress, without the benefits that flow *only* from the discretionary time of its employees; that is, if employees have no discretionary time, the organization will be denied their creativity, innovation, initiative, et cetera. The long-term penalty to me is that organizational life becomes a living death in which all I do is react to problems created by others, and I never have time to create and innovate and initiate on my own.

WHAT to do, then? Given the ongoing requirement of constantly maintaining the interconnected relationships among my boss, peers, and staff, how did I extricate myself from the mess I was in two years ago?

Although it is imperative that we manage all three relationships concurrently, we have to *start* somewhere. I started by eliminating subordinate-imposed time. There are two reasons for starting this way. One reason is that subordinate-imposed time does not belong in my schedule. The second is that some drastic changes had to be made quickly, and making such changes can make other people nervous. I didn't want to make anybody nervous, but if I had to do so, prudence dictated that they be the people with the least power to retaliate. Subordinates cannot impose extra monkeys on me without my cooperation, but bosses and peers can and will do so if I ignore their requirements in order to acquire some time to get my recovery jump-started.

So I began by eliminating subordinate-imposed time. That gave me an equal amount of discretionary time (since self-imposed time is the sum of discretionary time plus subordinate-imposed time), which I used to begin my managerial recovery process.

At the "Managing Management Time" seminar I heard an interesting story to illustrate the process. It's the story of two fellows running side by side through the woods, being chased by a bear. The bear was gaining. One fellow said to the other, "If I had my running shoes I could run a little faster." The other fellow replied, "I still don't think you could outrun the bear," to which came the retort, "I don't have to outrun the bear. I just have to outrun you!"

I found that even though you get a step ahead, the bear is still there! In my case, eliminating subordinate-imposed time gave me that extra step, but other demands on my time still existed, panting close behind: demands from my boss and peers, and legitimate requests from my staff. But the newly gained discretionary time gave me some room to get a handle on those other demands.

Once I got that little seed of discretionary time, I planted it carefully and made it grow. First, with my boss, I took time to figure out how to do my work in a way to build her confidence to the point where she began allowing me more and more discretion.

For example, there are many areas of my work where I previously could take no action until I checked with her first; she wanted to know my plans in advance so she could have a chance to forestall mistakes I might make.

All that checking with her took a lot of time for both of us. Since then, however, my record of success in those same areas has lowered her anxieties to the point where I am allowed to handle them on my own and inform her of what I did afterward in my quarterly report. This saves both of us a lot of time. In other words, I used my newly gained discretionary time in a way that gave me (and her!) even more discretionary time.

I followed a similar approach with my peers. In the past I had been relying solely on the authority of my position to get things done because I was too busy to deal with situations in more productive ways. And I paid for it. But once I got some discretionary time, I spent some of it building my relationships with people in the system and I found that the more rapport we had the more they would do for me with less effort on my part.

Again, just a short example will illustrate the process. In the past, if I urgently needed something from a staff person, the best I could get was routine, by-the-book effort ("Fill out the form and we'll go to work on it").

But in recent months I have invested some discretionary time in building better relationships with them. Now when I need something urgently I get their wholehearted support and it takes less of my time to get it—this from the very same system I used to criticize as bureaucratic, unwieldy, and unresponsive. Again, as with my boss, I have invested discretionary time to create even more discretionary time. In my dealings with the system I have learned that however inept it may be, the people who operate it can make it do wonders for me if they will. So rather than criticizing and resenting the imperfect system, I practice this philosophy: *It is better to strike a straight blow with a crooked stick than spend my whole life trying to straighten the darn thing out.*

Likewise with my people. As you now all too well know, in the space of a single morning (that "famous" Monday morning) I returned their monkeys to them and, in the process, converted several days of subordinate-imposed time into an equal amount of discretionary time. Then I began coaching my people along toward greater self-reliance. Every incremental increase in their self-reliance meant an equivalent increase in my discretionary time and in their morale. (There is a high correlation between self-reliance and morale.)

I now clearly measure my success by what I am able to get my people to do, not what I do myself. Fortunately, my boss measures me that way as well. And I am happy to report that I will soon be taking over a larger area of responsibility. I feel great, and I've been told I even look better than ever. Although I'm still busy, I no longer feel the pressed-for-time anxiety that I once did. The physical and emotional distress that were my constant companions before I learned monkey management are now just bad memories.

This all came about because I have learned to think differently about my work. My mentality has changed from that of a *do-er* to that of a *manager*. As such, I have not only learned the practice of monkey management, but also I have learned to replace the psychological rewards of *doing* with the rewards of *managing*, namely, deriving satisfaction from what my people do and being recognized, paid, and promoted accordingly.

What encouraged me most was seeing how my people responded to my new management style and how much their productivity and morale improved. Their performance enabled me to build a high degree of confidence in them, which meant that in many cases my involvement in a project amounted to little more than ratifying what they were doing.

The improved relationship with my staff was the first step in reversing the *vicious* cycle I was in and creating a *vital* cycle which, like the vicious one, is enormously powerful and feeds on itself. As my people responded to my improved management style, their productivity and morale improved, causing me to be less anxious about their work and allowing me to give them more freedom, thus releasing my time to invest elsewhere. I invested some of my newly found time with my boss, causing her anxieties to diminish and allowing her to give me more freedom. I also invested some time in improving my relationships with the people in the "system" to the point where I got more done in less time. I especially had time to better manage our customer and supplier relationships that are so key to our long-term survival.

Finally, one day, the vital cycle gave me a small surplus of that rare and precious commodity—discretionary time. I used that surplus time to begin pursuing (for the first time in a long time) some of the discretionary activities on my own agenda that make managerial life worthwhile. In other words, I began to do some manag*ing* instead of just being manag*ed*.

The Ultimate Conversion

In the past, I spent much of my time fighting fires; now I can prevent most of the fires by spending just a little time in advance. In the past, I spent a great deal of my time reacting to other people; now I spend a great deal of my time in proactive measures. These include doing some advance planning for a change so we can do the right things the right way the first time instead of having to do them over so often.

I came to realize that when people throughout the organization are given responsibility for managing their own monkeys, it's hard to tell who's a worker and who's a manager because everyone is committed to doing what it takes to do the best job possible.

Besides the changes in my own personal and professional life, I have begun to share my learnings with others I know—especially those time-pressed individuals who never seem to have enough time for their work, family, or friends. I help them to see the dynamics of monkey management and to become monkey managers in the zoo of their choice. This new way of life has changed my life and the lives of those around me.

Finally, perhaps the greatest lesson I have learned about monkey management, at work and at home, is that there are always more monkeys clamoring for attention than we have time to manage. Unless we are extremely careful which ones we accept responsibility for, it is very easy to wind up caring for the wrong monkeys while the really important ones are starving for lack of attention. If we thoughtlessly try to handle all of them, our efforts will be diluted to the point where none of them are healthy.

I hope this monkey tale will help you as much as it has helped me, which is enormously. I am constantly reminded of its benefits. For example, as I write these final words, I am alone in my office. My door is open. And as I glance at the new photograph of my family, I notice one major change: I'M NOW IN THE PICTURE!

The
End

:01 *Praisings*

We would like to give a public praising to a number of important people who played key roles in making this book a reality:

Robert Nelson, a very talented writer and vice-president of product development for Blanchard Training and Development, Inc. (BTD), for his assistance with the writing, editing, and coordination of this book.

Eleanor Terndrup, secretary extraordinaire, for her tireless effort in typing numerous drafts of this book over a four-year period.

William Oncken III and *Ramona Neel* of the William Oncken Corporation, for their invaluable assistance in editing the manuscript and helping to keep the content consistent with the "Managing Management Time" seminar.

George Heaton of Blanchard Training and Development, Canada, for providing the original spark from which this project grew.

Margret McBride for being our literary agent and providing constant support.

All the folks at William Morrow and Company, Inc., particularly *Larry Hughes*, *Al Marchioni*, our editor *Pat Golbitz*, and her assistant, *Jill Hamilton*, for continuing to believe in *The One Minute Manager Library* and supporting this addition to it.

Jim Ballard for his creative energy around "Rescuers Anonymous," and *Stephen Karpman*, for defining the term "rescuer" for us.

Paul Hersey for teaching us some of the lessons from Little League.

Marjorie Blanchard, *Margaret Oncken*, and *Alice Burrows* for their constant love and support throughout the peaks and valleys of our lives.

About the Authors

Kenneth Blanchard, co-developer of the One Minute Manager and Situational Leadership, is an internationally known author, educator, consultant/trainer, and professor of leadership and organization behavior at the University of Massachusetts, Amherst. He has written extensively in the fields of leadership, motivation, and managing change, including the ground-breaking *One Minute Manager Library* series, co-authored with some of the top management thinkers in the country, *The Power of Ethical Management*, co-authored with Dr. Norman Vincent Peale, and the widely used and acclaimed Prentice-Hall text *Management of Organizational Behavior*, co-authored with Paul Hersey, now in its fifth edition.

Dr. Blanchard received his B.A. in government and philosophy from Cornell University, an M.A. in sociology and counseling from Colgate University, and a Ph.D. in educational administration and management from Cornell University, where he presently serves on the Board of Trustees.

As chairman of the board of Blanchard Training and Development, Inc., a San Diego-based human-resource-development company he co-founded with his wife, Marjorie, Dr. Blanchard has trained over two hundred thousand managers and his approaches to management have been incorporated into many *Fortune 500* companies as well as numerous fast-growing entrepreneurial companies.

The late **William Oncken, Jr.,** was one of the most articulate spokesmen in the field of management. After his graduation from Princeton in 1934, Bill learned from practical experience that a manager's ability to generate and profitably use discretionary time is crucial to his career competitiveness and to his organization's ability to survive and prosper in our free-enterprise system. He translated his observations and practical experience into his internationally known MANAGING MANAGEMENT TIME and MANAGING MANAGERIAL INITIATIVE seminars; his revolutionary article "Managing Management Time: Who's Got the Monkey?" (co-authored with Donald Wass); and his recently published book, *Managing Management Time*, destined to become a classic of management literature.

Mr. Oncken founded his own company in 1960. Based in Dallas, The William Oncken Corporation continues to provide his high-quality management development programs, teaching his unique managerial philosophy and perspective.

For more than three decades the fruits of his creative genius, his MANAGING MANAGEMENT TIME seminar, has helped managers generate and fully utilize that most precious managerial commodity: discretionary time.

The One Minute Manager Meets the Monkey is adapted from and emphasizes the "staff" strategy of "Oncken's Management Molecule."

When it comes to management time *Hal Burrows* speaks with authority. His experience at two *Fortune 500* companies and fifteen years of running his own consulting firm as well as his ability to communicate his insights with wit and flair have made him a very popular speaker on the subject of management and negotiating. Since 1973 his face-to-face experience with thousands of managers at all levels from hundreds of private companies and government agencies has enabled him to help them become more successful in their careers. In addition to speaking at conventions and other major meetings, Burrows presents two highly acclaimed seminars: Managing Management Time, and Managing Negotiations Under Pressure.

Hal is also a successful entrepreneur in the area of commercial real estate development in Raleigh, North Carolina (P.O. Box 52070, Raleigh, NC 27612, 919-787-9769), where he and his family reside.

Services Available

Ken Blanchard, Bill Oncken III, Hal Burrows, and their organizations work closely together in helping other organizations develop more skillful managers. Providing books such as this is only one of their services; complementary services have been designed to help managers personally acquire the skills described in *The One Minute Manager Meets the Monkey*.

Services available include: presentations at conventions and major meetings, seminars ranging from two to five days, ongoing consultation, and learning materials (including self-assessment instruments, books, micro-computer programs, and audio and video programs).

If you would like further information about any of these services you may contact:

For Ken Blanchard's products and services,

Blanchard Training and Development, Inc.
125 State Place
Escondido, CA 92025
(800) 854-1013 or
(619) 489-5005 (in California)

For Bill Oncken's and Hal Burrows's products and services,

The William Oncken Corporation
Suite 408
8344 East R.L. Thornton Freeway
Dallas, TX 75228
(214) 328-1867

The One Minute Manager Builds High Performing Teams

Kenneth Blanchard
Donald Carew
Eunice Parisi-Carew

The Symbol

The One Minute Manager's symbol—a one minute readout from the face of a modern digital watch—is intended to remind each of us to take a minute out of our day to look into the faces of the people we manage. And to realize that *they* are our most important resources.

Introduction

Never before in the history of the workplace has the concept of teamwork been more important to the functioning of successful organizations. With the rapid social, technological and informational changes that are occurring, our society is faced with stresses never before encountered. Our organizations are more complex and more competitive. No longer can we depend upon a few peak performers to rise to the top to lead. If we are to survive we must figure out ways to tap into the creativity and potential of people at all levels.

Couple these changes with a shifting population, a change in values and a change in the traditional work ethic, and you have a rising demand for new organizational structures and a new definition of leadership. People are demanding more. They want fulfillment as well as good pay.

As a result, there has been a movement toward participation and involvement so strong that it's called the *Third Revolution* in management practices. A new organizational structure is coming into its own—the team which increases ownership and commitment, unleashes creativity and builds skills. Today's leader must be an enabler of people and a facilitator of groups — not only as an effective group leader but as an effective group member as well.

The team of Blanchard Training and Development (BTD) has been doing a great deal of work in the area of high-performing teams for the past ten years, and founding BTD associates, Don Carew and Eunice Parisi-Carew, have spearheaded that work. Don and Eunice have been close friends and colleagues for over 20 years and we have spent countless hours working together on the implementation of the concepts in this book. I believe the concepts taught through parable in *The One Minute Manager Builds High Performing Teams* present a clear map for managing the journey to more productive and satisfying teams.

As you'll see, our work on teams is well integrated with Situational Leadership® II *(Leadership and the One Minute Manager)*. In fact, improvements made to the Situational Leadership® model were stimulated by our research on group development, and I am indebted to Don and Eunice for advocating many of those changes. Their commitment to creating opportunities for people to have more satisfying and productive lives and for organizations to be more caring, creative and successful is at the heart of their work.

The ideas in this latest edition to THE ONE MINUTE MANAGER LIBRARY have been shared with thousands of people in all types of teams and organizations and these concepts never fail to have a powerful impact. I hope this book is as informative and helpful to you and your teams as it has been to them.

Kenneth Blanchard, Ph.D.
Co-Author
The One Minute Manager

To our mothers

Dorothy, Marjorie and Jenny,

who gave us our first lessons in

empowerment and

loving others.

Contents

The One Minute Manager Receives a Call 11
The Problem 13
The Importance of Groups 16
Characteristics of a High Performing Team 19
The Importance of Vision 26
Diagnosis 28
Understanding Group Dynamics 31
Stage 1: Orientation 35
Stage 2: Dissatisfaction 41
Stage 4: Production 51
Stage 3: Resolution 58
Changes in Productivity and Morale 65
Adaptability 68
Four Leadership Styles 70
Task and Maintenance Functions 75
Teaching Someone Else 77
Using the Concepts 80
Answering the Questions 83
Managing the Journey to Empowerment 85
When to Change One's Leadership Style 89
Regression 96
Process Observation 97
Understanding Group Dynamics 101
The Manager as Educator 102
The New One Minute Managers 106
Sharing It With Others 108
Praisings 112
About the Authors 114
Services Available 118

THE One Minute Manager was staring out his office window. It was still his favorite place to come when he wanted to think. As he gazed across the grounds, the sound of the phone ringing startled him. Coming back to reality, he walked over to the coffee table in front of his couch and picked up the receiver. When he was in his office the One Minute Manager liked to answer his own phone.

The voice on the other end of the phone was Dan Brockway, the director of training at a large chemical company.

"How's it going, Dan?" asked the One Minute Manager.

"Just fine," said Dan, "but I do need some advice on our Essentials of Management course."

The Essentials of Management course was a new training program that Dan was teaching at his company that focused on the key skills managers needed to be effective in the 1990's. He had spent some time with the One Minute Manager while he was designing the course and was enthusiastic about the commitment of his company's top management to expose all their managers to the best management thinking available.

"Didn't you just finish the first session?"

"I sure did," said Dan. "And the reviews were great with one exception. A young woman, Maria Sanchez, who coordinates our customer service programs, has some serious concerns about the usefulness of some of the materials. In fact, she wrote me a letter about her concerns and distributed copies to key people."

"What were her concerns?" asked the One Minute Manager.

"SHE said all the concepts taught focused primarily on managing people one-on-one and, as such, are limited. She claims that 50 to 90 percent of most managers' time is spent in some form of group activity with two or more people, and yet our course doesn't emphasize teamwork at all. Therefore, we are not providing help in one of the most significant areas of a manager's job."

"That's interesting," said the One Minute Manager. "Tell me more."

"She also thinks the concepts of One Minute Management are based too much on control," said Dan. "The manager sets the goals, the manager gives praisings and the manager delivers reprimands. Let me quote from her letter:

'We need managers who can foster teamwork, facilitate group problem solving and focus the group's attention and enthusiasm on continuous improvement. In today's world, group productivity is often more important than individual task accomplishment. The success of individual managers should depend on how well the manager's group improves in quality and productivity on a continuous basis. Systems that can pit team player against team player must be changed so that the priority of each team member becomes the accomplishment of the group's mission. To do that, managers must give up a great deal of control to their people. When that occurs, a feeling of group ownership is created and the group develops pride that comes from producing high-quality accomplishments. You will never hear 'It's not my job' in an organization committed to teamwork.' "

"She sounds like quite a person," said the One Minute Manager. "How can I help you?"

"Could you dictate a response to her letter? She could really disrupt our whole program if we don't get her on track."

"I don't think she's off track," said the One Minute Manager. "In fact, I'd like to meet her. Sounds like she is really aware of some important issues. I think that One Minute Management principles are sound, but I would agree with her that if you teach those principles without any attention to group skills, you have given managers only half the story. Let's have lunch tomorrow at 12:30 in the main dining room of City Hotel so I can explain to you why I think Maria is on the *right* track."

"That would be fine with me," said Dan. "Sounds like I still have some things to learn."

"Don't feel like the Lone Ranger," said The One Minute Manager. "See you tomorrow!"

THE next day at lunch, the One Minute Manager immediately got to the reason for the meeting.

"Dan, I used to be frustrated at work even though I knew all kinds of effective management techniques. For a long time I didn't know why I was frustrated. I finally realized one day, just as your friend Maria has realized, that most of my job was not supervising and working with people one–on–one but, instead, it involved working with people in groups."

"I thought a lot about what you said last night," commented Dan. "So you really don't believe that we spend much time supervising people individually?"

"No, I don't," said the One Minute Manager. "In fact, most managers spend less than 30 percent of their time directly supervising their people individually. They spend most of their time in group meetings dealing with their people or with peers and their boss, or with people external to their organization such as customers or suppliers. When I first realized that, I decided that I'd better learn something about groups and how they operate."

"Could you tell me what you learned?" asked Dan.

"First of all," said the One Minute Manager, "when groups are operating effectively they can solve more complex problems, make better decisions, release more creativity and do more to build individual skills and commitment than individuals working alone."

"Can't they also destroy productivity?" wondered Dan.

"They sure can," said the One Minute Manager, "if they're not managed well. That's why today's leader must be an enabler of people and a facilitator of groups.

"What else did you learn?"

"Secondly, all groups are unique," continued the One Minute Manager.

"They are all dynamic, complex, ever-changing, living systems that—just like individuals—have behavior patterns and lives of their own."

"How do groups differ from one another?" asked Dan.

"Well, there are the obvious differences of size, purpose and individual members, but an important difference that is often overlooked is in their stage of development," said the One Minute Manager. "All groups go through similar stages as they grow from a collection of individuals when they first get together to a smoothly functioning, effective team."

"Do you mean all groups go through the same stages of development no matter what their purpose or size or how frequently they meet?" asked Dan.

"In general, yes, but primarily I'm thinking about teams that interact face-to-face on a regular basis, have a relatively constant membership of between two to fifteen members and are working together on a common task or problem. They can be ongoing work units, special task forces or committees with short-term objectives, athletic teams or even social groups or families," answered the One Minute Manager.

"That certainly would include most of the groups to which I've belonged," said Dan. "But what about larger groups?"

"The same stages can be observed in larger groups as well," said the One Minute Manager, "but when groups get larger than 15 or 20 people, they become less effective and should divide into smaller units to accomplish tasks or solve problems."

"That makes sense," said Dan. "Can you tell me how you would describe an effective team?"

"BEFORE I answer that," said the One Minute Manager, "I'd like you to think of a time when you were part of an outstanding team or group. Think of a team that produced a high-quality result and one to which you were proud to belong."

"There haven't been many like that," replied Dan, "but the design team I've been working with for this Essentials of Management course comes close. Five of us have been working together for the past six months and we feel good about what we are accomplishing."

"What I'd like you to do," said the One Minute Manager, "is think about that team and make a list of the factors you think have contributed to its effectiveness. I have a phone call to make, so let's get back together in 10 minutes and see what you have on your list."

"Fine," said Dan as he began to make notes.

After the phone call the One Minute Manager asked Dan to show him his list.

"It's not very long," remarked Dan, "but I think it describes some of the main characteristics of the effective groups with which I have worked." Dan had seven items on his list:

1. I know what I have to do and the team's goals are clear.
2. Everyone takes some responsibility for leadership.
3. There is active participation by everyone.
4. I feel appreciated and supported by others.
5. Team members listen when I speak.
6. Different opinions are respected.
7. We enjoy working together and we have fun.

"That's a good start, Dan," said the One Minute Manager, "and it's right on target with what I've observed happening in high-performing teams. I've come up with the acronym PERFORM, which describes the essentials of an effective team. I've had it put on a small card so people can keep it with them at all times." With that, the One Minute Manager reached into his coat pocket to get a card and then handed it to Dan. It read:

Characteristics of High Performing Teams

Purpose
Empowerment
Relationships And Communication
Flexibility
Optimal Performance
Recognition And Appreciation
Morale

"That's catchy," said Dan. "I'd be interested in how you describe those variables."

"Sure," said the One Minute Manager as he handed Dan a questionnaire. "Here's a rating form that I put together which describes each of the characteristics and permits you to evaluate a team to which you belong. As you read it think about your design team."

Dan began to read:

High PERFORMing Team Rating Form
Think how your team would rate on a scale of 1–5
(1 = low; 5 = high)

Purpose
1. Members can describe and are committed to a common purpose.
2. Goals are clear, challenging and relevant to purpose.
3. Strategies for achieving goals are clear.
4. Individual roles are clear.

Empowerment
5. Members feel a personal and collective sense of power.
6. Members have access to necessary skills and resources.
7. Policies and practices support team objectives.
8. Mutual respect and willingness to help each other is evident.

Relationships and Communication
9. Members express themselves openly and honestly.
10. Warmth, understanding and acceptance is expressed.
11. Members listen actively to each other.
12. Differences of opinion and perspective are valued.

Flexibility
13. Members perform different roles and functions as needed.
14. Members share responsibility for team leadership and team development.
15. Members are adaptable to changing demands.
16. Various ideas and approaches are explored.

Optimal Productivity
17. Output is high.
18. Quality is excellent.
19. Decision making is effective.
20. Clear problem-solving process is apparent.

Recognition and Appreciation
21. Individual contributions are recognized and appreciated by leader and other members.
22. Team accomplishments are recognized by members.
23. Group members feel respected.
24. Team contributions are valued and recognized by the organization.

Morale
25. Individuals feel good about their membership on the team.
26. Individuals are confident and motivated.
27. Members have a sense of pride and satisfaction about their work.
28. There is a strong sense of cohesion and team spirit.

"Thanks," said Dan as he looked up from the rating form. "This is really helpful. I would rate our design team 4 or 5 on every one of those scales.

"We had a clear purpose, we felt empowered, our relationships and communication were good, we were flexible, our quality and performance were high, we felt appreciated and recognized and our morale was strong. It's sad, though, that I can't say that about most of the groups with which I've worked."

"Yes, it is sad," said the One Minute Manager. "Wouldn't it be wonderful if all of our work units could describe themselves as PERFORM teams."

"It sure would," Dan replied. "If that were true, morale and productivity would go off the chart. I saw a poster on a school bulletin board that captured the importance of developing a team. It stated:

*

NONE OF US

IS AS SMART

AS ALL OF US

*

"How true that is," said the One Minute Manager. "And if we acted on that belief, think what a difference it would make in how people feel about themselves and their work. And that's what people are demanding today. They want fulfillment as well as good pay."

"Are any of the PERFORM characteristics more important than any other?"

"No," said the One Minute Manager. "They all have different functions. An effective team starts with a clear *purpose*. The hoped-for end results are *optimal productivity* and good *morale*. The means to those ends are *empowerment, relationships* and *communication, flexibility* and *recognition* and *appreciation*.

"So the first thing an effective leader needs to do is create a common purpose or vision that helps point the team in the right direction," suggested Dan.

"That's essential," said the One Minute Manager. "A common vision tells people why they are working together. It creates meaning and helps everyone row in the same direction.

I recently read a beautiful story that relates to the importance of purpose. Two workers were hammering on a piece of granite with a sledgehammer. When asked what he was doing, the first worker said, 'I'm trying to crack this granite.'"

"When asked the same question, the second worker said, 'I'm part of a team building a cathedral.'"

"Vision inspires performance and commitment," said the One Minute Manager. "Knowing where you are headed and having everything move in the same direction is critical. But alignment around a shared vision or purpose is just the beginning of the road to a high-performing team."

"That's what I was afraid of," said Dan thoughtfully. "Knowing how a high-performing team functions is helpful, but how groups get to that point is a mystery to me."

"Well," replied the One Minute Manager, "it isn't by accident! And it's not as much of a mystery as it once was. We have learned a lot about group dynamics, group development and group leadership over the past 40 years. It is just that most organizations haven't put that knowledge to use very effectively. We have only recently realized how powerful teams can be in improving productivity, quality and human satisfaction in organizations."

"**I'M** sold," said Dan. "What do I need to do to be an effective team leader and how can I help my people over time?"

"The whole process of developing a high-performing team involves three major skills on the part of team leaders and team members as well. The first is *Diagnosis*, the second is *Adaptability* and the third is *Empowerment*.

"Let's start with Diagnosis," continued the One Minute Manager. "Understanding the dynamics and the behavioral patterns that exist in groups is essential if you want to facilitate the group's development and productivity. I have found that the skillful leader or group member must do more than listen and talk. Perhaps most important is the skill of observing the group in action. Groups are extremely complex. As you increase the size of the group, the number of interaction patterns or subgroups flows geometrically so that with two people in a group there is just one subgroup. With four people in a team it jumps to 11 subgroups and with eight people it goes to 247 subgroups. Because of this complexity it is important that we have ways to observe the group that help us make sense of what is going on."

"I see!" exclaimed Dan. "Thinking about it that way makes it seem almost impossible to ever make sense of what goes on in a team."

"It's not impossible at all, Dan," said the One Minute Manager. "We have already talked about what a high-performing team looks like and if we keep the PERFORM model in mind we have a sense of how we would like our teams to be working. Even though groups are complex, there are a number of things we can observe that influence a group's morale and productivity. One of the first steps for effective group leaders, as well as members, is to become effective observers and participants at the same time."

"How do I get started learning more about groups?"

"One way is to just start observing various groups. What I'd like you to do sometime early next week, if you have some free time, is to come on over to our company and sit in and watch what goes on in some different groups. I'll check, but I'm sure they won't mind an observer. I'll want you to watch for two kinds of things going on in the groups."

The One Minute Manager pulled out his note pad and drew a diagram.

Elements of Group Interaction

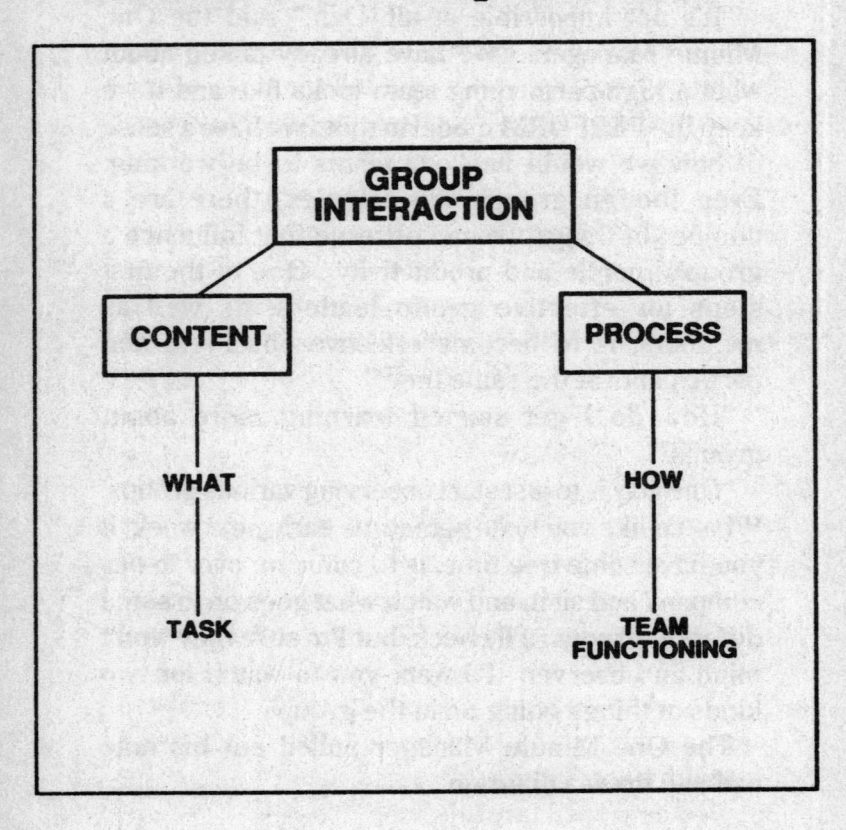

```
          GROUP
       INTERACTION
         /      \
   CONTENT      PROCESS
      |            |
    WHAT          HOW
      |            |
    TASK         TEAM
              FUNCTIONING
```

"The *content* is what the group is doing—its task," said the One Minute Manager. "For example, if later today someone asked you what went on during our lunch together, you would tell them we talked about the importance and characteristics of groups. We were all trained in school to track content and ignore process. Content describes *what* was done at a meeting, while process depicts *how* the team functions. The process is what is happening to and between group members, like leadership struggle, communication and the ways decisions are made. You have to focus on it to see it. Unfortunately we often pay little attention to process, yet it is critically important because process affects outcome. Group leaders who do not legitimize looking at group process can become blind to why people are unhappy even though the agenda at the meeting is getting accomplished. When that happens, 'I should have said' meetings begin to crop up in the hallways, bathrooms, stairwells, elevators and parking lots."

"This list is a helpful reminder to me whenever I am observing a group's process." The One Minute Manager wrote on his note pad again. When he finished he ripped off the sheet. It read:

*

WHAT TO OBSERVE IN GROUPS

- *Communication and participation*
- *Decision making*
- *Conflict*
- *Leadership*
- *Goals and roles*
- *Group norms*
- *Problem solving*
- *Climate/tone*

*

"*Communication* and *participation*," continued the One Minute Manager, "are about who talks to whom? Who is left out? Who talks most often? etc. *Decision making* involves how a group goes about selecting a course of action—majority rule, consensus, lack of response, etc. *Conflict* is inevitable and necessary in reaching effective and creative solutions for problems. How is conflict handled in the group—avoidance, compromise, competition, collaboration, etc. *Leadership* is all about who is influencing whom. To be effective a team must be clear on its *roles* (who does what?) and *goals* (what are they trying to accomplish?). *Norms* are the assumptions or expectations held by group members that govern the kinds of behaviors that are appropriate or inappropriate in the group. They are the ground rules which regulate the group's behavior. Which norms are most obvious in this group? Effective *problem solving* involves identifying and formulating the problem, generating alternative solutions, analyzing consequences, action planning and evaluation. How does the group solve problems? And finally, *group climate* refers to the feeling or tone of the group—how pleasant it seems."

"That's a lot to be watching," said Dan, "if you are also a member of the group."

"That's true," said the One Minute Manager. "But all team leaders, and group members as well, need to practice the skill of being a participant observer."

"What is that?" asked Dan.

"That means being fully engaged in the content or the agenda, whatever it is, and yet being able to step back and observe the dynamics which are occurring in the group at the same time," said the One Minute Manager.

"So, for example, if we are making a decision I need to be involved in the decision itself, as well as be aware of how the decision is being made," replied Dan.

"Absolutely right," said the One Minute Manager. "If a decision is railroaded through by one or two members and not checked for agreement, you may find yourself up a creek without a paddle and have little support when you go to implement the decision."

"I've certainly seen that happen," smiled Dan.

"It sounds tough, though, to be both participant and observer."

"It is at first, but the skill of participant observer is just like any other human skill. It can be learned and practiced until it is second nature," replied the One Minute Manager.

"Sounds like a challenge," said Dan.

"Yes it is," said the One Minute Manager. "It takes concentration and practice. That starts with learning to observe and track the dynamics which occur in a group setting. Understanding those dynamics is the key to diagnosing a group's functioning and the stage of its development."

DAN got to do some group observation on Monday afternoon. The One Minute Manager arranged for him to sit in on a performance appraisal task force chaired by Ron Tillman, the company's chief operating officer.

Dan arrived a few moments early for the meeting on Monday to find all members already there drinking coffee and chatting amiably. Smiling, he joined the conversation, which ended promptly at 2:00 p.m., when a jovial-looking man in his early fifties entered the room. He immediately went to Dan and stuck out his hand. "Good afternoon. I'm Ron Tilman. Glad you could make it."

After exchanging greetings with team members and introducing Dan to the rest of the group, Ron started the meeting.

"I'm excited about this task force. I see this as a very important group that could have a major impact on our organization. We are charged with revising our performance appraisal system so that it is more helpful in creating higher levels of motivation and performance throughout our organization. A successful system should help all people set clearer goals, know how they are doing in relation to those goals, and provide a framework for providing reviews and recognition for accomplishment. It should help managers be more effective in developing competence and commitment among their staff."

"My hope," continued Ron, "is that what we develop will help this company be a win-win organization for our people and for our customers. It is a complex task and we will need to learn how to work together, be open in our communication, share leadership and decision-making responsibilities and build ourselves into a high-performing team."

"We have a one-month window to accomplish this task. The first step is to clarify our mission and to come to agreement on the goals and the roles each of you will play in its accomplishment."

Ron proceeded to write the roles and goals of the group on a flipchart at the head of the table.

Dan was struck with the efficiency of the meeting opening, but a bit disturbed about the directness of Tilman. He observed the eagerness of the group and, although he felt their expectations were a bit unrealistic (such as the fact that they thought they could accomplish the task in one month), he was surprised that Tilman did not encourage their enthusiasm as the meeting progressed, but instead kept pulling them back to the task.

After the meeting Dan approached Tilman. "Well, what did you think about our first meeting?" asked Tilman.

"To be honest, I'm not sure," replied Dan. "I liked the way you gave them the big picture and how you got things started. But I also noticed people expressing some concern about the task, and some members seemed tense."

"Yes," said Ron. "Whenever you have a new group, members are concerned about how they fit into the group. This causes some caution and mistrust between group members. You can expect a combination of caution and excitement at first. What did you think about my leadership style?"

"Well," smiled Dan, "you were a bit direct. More so than I would have expected, but it seemed to work. It did not hamper their enthusiasm. In fact, they seemed somewhat relieved."

"Do you think they have a firm foundation to start from?" questioned Tilman.

"They sure do," replied Dan. "I think they have an overall sense of purpose and are beginning to understand their goals and roles."

"That's what I wanted," smiled Tilman. "All new groups need to have a sense of purpose as well as some clarity about group goals and individual roles. I'm pleased you saw that happening. Thanks for joining us."

When Dan went to see the One Minute Manager later that afternoon he was asked, "Well, how was your visit with the performance review task force?"

"It was fine, I guess," said Dan. "Your comments about creating a common vision sure held up. Ron spent some time outlining a purpose and his hopes. Everyone seemed to be eager, but they needed some sense of direction. Ron clearly provided that kind of leadership. If that's your secret to building a high-performing team then I got it—the leader should take charge."

"It's not quite that simple," said the One Minute Manager. "Remember, that was the first meeting of that task force and the members needed to be clear on their mission, goals and responsibilities. All teams go through stages in their development and you've just described what is pretty typical for a group in its first stage. I call that the *Orientation* Stage or Stage 1. This card will summarize what's going on in Stage 1."

When the One Minute Manager handed Dan the card he read:

Group Development Stage 1—Orientation

Characteristics

- Feeling moderately eager with high expectations
- Feeling some anxiety: Where do I fit? What is expected of me?
- Testing the situation and central figures
- Depending on authority and hierarchy
- Needing to find a place and establish oneself

"The Orientation Stage reminds me of how dogs behave when they first meet. They run up eagerly but, before they play, they get very cautious and check each other out. I call that the sniffing stage. As the team progresses it will move into other stages."

"I see," laughed Dan still thinking about the dogs. "Then you're saying that there are several stages and that things change as the team grows."

"That's exactly right. Before we talk about any of the other stages, I'd like you to visit another group in our company that is further along than Ron's group. We have a productivity improvement team that's been meeting for a couple of weeks trying to look at the issue of customer complaints and billing problems. Let me find out when they are having their next meeting and ask them to let you observe."

"Sounds good," said Dan. "I'll call you tomorrow."

"No, I'll find out right now," said the One Minute Manager as he picked up the phone and called Susan Schaefer. "Susan," he said, "I have a young man up here who wants to learn about high-performing teams and I wonder if he could observe the next meeting of your billing task force."

Dan could not hear her, but Susan said, "I suppose he could observe, but he won't learn much about effective teams if he looks at us."

"THAT'S just the point," said the One Minute Manager. "I want him to see how groups grow and develop, and from what you've told me, your team is in the second stage most groups encounter: *Dissatisfaction*, or Stage 2."

"I guess you're right," replied Susan. "We're meeting at 2:00 p.m. on Wednesday. Have him meet me in my office about 1:45 p.m. and I'll brief him."

"Good afternoon," said Dan when he met Susan in the hall outside her office. "The One Minute Manager sent me down here to observe your task force."

"Right," said Susan. "We are having our fourth meeting in a few minutes. The task force has four people from shipping, two from accounting, three from sales and the director of the computer systems office. We're working on improving our billing and accounts receivable process and reducing customer complaints. We're having a hard time pinpointing the problem areas. Why don't you join the meeting but sit a little apart from the others and just observe."

Dan sat in the corner as the others gathered. Susan called the meeting to order about 2:05 p.m. but one of the people said they should wait until everyone was there. Another person left unexpectedly at that point and went down the hall. By 2:10 p.m. everyone was there and Susan opened by saying, "This is our fourth meeting and, although we have set goals of increasing billing accuracy and reducing customer complaints, we haven't agreed upon clear strategies and action plans to accomplish either task."

"That's not true," responded Sam, a member of the sales staff. "We give the accounting department accurate information on our orders but they can't seem to keep track of the information."

Immediately one of the accounting staff and the computer systems director joined in and for a few minutes everyone was talking at once. The session seemed chaotic and Dan soon lost track of what topic was being discussed.

After about five more minutes Susan rapped on the table and said, "Hold it. This isn't getting us anywhere. Everyone is talking at once. I want one person to talk at a time. Let's go around the room and in one sentence I'd like each of you to identify what you think the most important issue is."

The process seemed to help clarify some of the issues. People still seemed frustrated, however, even though it was clear that they were beginning to understand some of the major areas of concern.

"Well, what did you think?" Susan asked Dan as they left the meeting about 3:30 p.m.

"I'm confused," he replied. "That session felt very uncomfortable to me. Everyone seemed frustrated and some people were even angry. When you focused on a task you took control and asked for their input. They seemed to be challenging you and each other or withdrawing from the group. And then you congratulated the group at the end even though you had criticized them earlier."

"I understand your confusion," said Susan. "Let's talk about it more later. I have another appointment right now."

"That session," thought Dan, "reminded me of a lot of the groups I've worked with over the years."

"It's why I don't like groups and meetings. It's why ...

*

SOME PEOPLE

REFER

TO MEETINGS

AS A PLACE

WHERE

YOU TAKE MINUTES

AND

WASTE HOURS

*

Dan laughed to himself as he thought about that statement. "I guess that's better than saying, 'A camel is a horse designed by a commitee,' although that fits my experience with groups."

Dan was still confused as he went back to the One Minute Manager's office to discuss his experience.

"That was quite a meeting," he said, as he went into the office. "What I'm most confused about is why you called that Stage 2. That group seemed less productive and less friendly than the group you said was at Stage 1."

"That's exactly right," chuckled the One Minute Manager, "and predictable. That's why we call it the *Dissatisfaction* Stage. It's what happens after the honeymoon is over. This card will describe what's going on in this stage."

As the One Minute Manager handed Dan another card, he began to read:

Group Development Stage 2—Dissatisfaction

Characteristics

- Experiencing a discrepancy between hopes and reality
- Feeling dissatisfied with dependence on authority
- Feeling frustrated: anger around goals, tasks and action plans
- Feeling incompetent and confused
- Reacting negatively toward leaders and other members
- Competing for power and/or attention
- Experiencing polarities: dependence/counter-dependence

"That's helpful," said Dan. "That stage just isn't very effective, is it?"

"Wait a minute," said the One Minute Manager. "You're jumping to conclusions and making a lot of assumptions. I said this was Stage 2, but I didn't say it was an unproductive stage. It's a stage that all groups go through on their way to being productive. It is a stage that is rarely, if ever, avoided."

"You mean to tell me," said Dan, "that all groups have to go through this bad stage or unproductive stage in order to get anywhere?"

"That's right," said the One Minute Manager. "But I wouldn't call it a 'bad' stage any more than I'd call an adolescent a bad person. It's just the process that we have to go through as the group develops. Although this stage is characterized by power struggles and conflict, it also is the seedbed of creativity and valuing differences."

"Well, it seemed to me," said Dan, "that, not only was productivity not very high but, people were feeling terrible. They weren't liking each other and the morale in the group was low."

"Yes," said the One Minute Manager, "that happens over and over again in groups. There's a dip in morale or commitment as people realize that the group's task is harder than they initially expected. As you read on the card, people get dissatisfied with the group's chairperson or often with each other. They often have negative reactions because the goals seem too high. They may have feelings of confusion or incompetence. As a result of those feelings, morale often takes a dip. In fact, some groups start in this stage. This is especially true when it's an undesirable task like downsizing in an organization. If team members are not there voluntarily or if the committee assignment just feels like extra work, then the group may start with low morale and low competence, that is, Stage 2. It is important, though, that you remember:

NO DEVELOPMENTAL STAGE IS BAD

EACH STAGE IS PART OF THE JOURNEY TOWARD PRODUCTION

"Groups need to work through the issues inherent in the Dissatisfaction Stage," continued the One Minute Manager. "They need to be encouraged to express their feelings of frustration and confusion so that those feelings can be dealt with and resolved."

"I'll have to take your word for it," said Dan. "But so much of my experience is similar to what I've just observed that I'm feeling depressed about the possibility of really applying some of your concepts to groups and teams."

"BEFORE we talk more, let's have you observe another group. It might give you some ideas about what might happen next as groups develop."

The shipping department's regular meeting was scheduled for 8:45 a.m. each Monday. Dan awoke early, curious about what the group he would be observing would be like. After a hurried breakfast he got in the car. Then it happened. The car would not start. Despite all his efforts the motor refused to turn over. Time was slipping by. Finally in desperation he called a taxi. By the time he reached the company, the shipping meeting had been in progress for ten minutes. Quietly he slipped in the door and sat in the back of the room. However, his entrance did not go unobserved. All 15 members stopped their work and each member in turn introduced him or herself and welcomed Dan. They wanted him to sit at the round table but Dan refused. Upon completion of the introductions, the group went back to work.

As Dan observed, he noted how enthusiastically they approached the task. They were working on a way to cut the time a certain procedure took by 15 percent. They pointed to the charts and graphs on the walls. Dan was fascinated at their system for tracking progress toward their 15 percent reduction goal and made a promise to explore this process further with the shipping department manager. One thing that puzzled him was: Who was leading the group?

He was totally baffled. The group worked quickly, sharing information and proposing ideas. People differed with each other, even argued, but always seemed to resolve their differences. There was joking and teasing among group members. At one time the group split into three subgroups to come up with a solution to a procedural issue. Then they joined together and reached consensus. The atmosphere was one of high energy and productivity. But who was the leader? There did not seem to be one. The group seemed to move as a unit with different people taking leadership at different times. Dan was puzzled.

At 10:15 a.m. a tall, serious-looking gentleman in his early thirties entered the room.

"Sorry I'm late. I had another commitment," he said.

The group responded with "hellos" and continued its work. The tall gentleman approached Dan.

"Hello. I'm Neil Henry. How are you?"

"Just fine," replied Dan.

"I'll speak with you later. I need to catch up on what's happened here so far in the meeting," said Neil.

Dan was curious about this new delinquent member and how the group would handle a new person. To his surprise, work proceeded at the same pace. Neil contributed ideas, occasionally reinforced and praised, or disagreed. His contributions were no different than others and were accepted in the same way.

At 10:45 a.m. the meeting ended. As they filed out the door, the members expressed pleasure that Dan had been able to join them. Dan was impressed. He had never been to a meeting where so much had been accomplished so smoothly and with such a positive attitude. It was as though the group acted as one unit and not a number of individuals. He couldn't help thinking of the analogy of a well-oiled machine where all parts were functioning in perfect harmony to produce a desired outcome.

His thoughts were interrupted as Neil approached.

"I hope you learned what you wanted," said Neil. "They're quite a group. We've been working together for two years. They really don't need me here anymore."

Dan's eyes widened. "Are you the department head?"

"Why yes," smiled Neil.

Dan stammered a bit. "That's the one thing I couldn't figure out."

"Oh," chuckled Neil. "I know it's different than what you are used to and it wasn't always that way. We've had our rough times. My goal has been to work myself out of a job gradually as the group developed and I'd say we're there, wouldn't you?"

"Absolutely," agreed Dan. "It's all making sense now. You have to change your leadership depending on the stage of development the group is in and the goal is to get the group to the point where they are, not only accomplishing the task efficiently but, operating effectively as a team."

"You've got it," replied Neil. "When you do that you will have a group in the *Production* Stage."

Following the meeting, Dan hurried to the One Minute Manager's office humming with excitement. "Is he in?" Dan asked.

"Yes, but he has somebody with him. He should be free shortly," smiled Dana, the One Minute Manager's executive assistant.

As he waited, Dan reflected on his experiences over the past few days and jotted down some notes:

1. Members on the performance appraisal committee were enthusiastic, yet concerned about how they fit in. They were in Stage 1: Orientation. They had little knowledge of the task. Ron Tilman used highly directive behavior to clarify the mission, set roles and goals and define tasks. There was little two-way interaction except at the end when he asked how people were feeling and if they understood the time lines and next steps.

2. Susan Schaefer's productivity group members were confused and disgruntled. They were in Stage 2: Dissatisfaction. They were making headway but it was slow. Sue was very assertive in the management of the group, but she also encouraged people to express their thoughts and opinions.

3. The shipping department was operating so smoothly and with such efficiency that the absence of Neil, the department head, seemed to have little impact. He said they were in the production stage. The group was enthusiastic and highly productive. Neil's contributions were no different from any other member's, but how did that group get there?

Dan pondered this question. Instinctively, he knew there was a piece missing. A group could not just move from a disgruntled group of individuals into such a synergistic, productive unit.

As he thought, the One Minute Manager appeared. "Hello, Dan, how's it going?"

Dan's excitement had now given way to a frown.

"You look puzzled," responded the One Minute Manager.

"Well, I am," said Dan. "You see, I witnessed a group getting started. The group leader was careful to lay out all the groundwork and provide direction. The next group I observed was moving slowly, accomplishing the task, but seemed to be very fragmented. More like the meetings I'm used to. Susan did not appear disturbed by this. She provided a lot of direction, both in terms of tasks and getting people to work together, and she listened patiently."

"Next I visited Neil's group. They were in the production stage. They seemed to have it all together. They were enjoying each other and the work and the group was managing itself. My question is: How did they get there? Did I miss something?"

"That you did," smiled the One Minute Manager. "You leap-frogged over an important stage in group development. You went straight from dissatisfaction to production. Before I talk about the missing stage, let me give you a summary card for Stage 4: Production." It read:

Group Development Stage 4—Production

Characteristics

- Feeling excited about participating in team activities
- Working collaboratively and interdependently with whole- and sub-groups
- Feeling team strength
- Showing high confidence in accomplishing tasks
- Sharing leadership
- Feeling positive about task successes
- Performing at high levels

"THAT certainly describes how Neil's group operated," said Dan. "Tell me about the stage I missed."

"That stage is called *Resolution*. It's the bridge between the dissatisfaction you witnessed in Susan's group and the efficiency and excitement in Neil's."

"What happens in that stage?" questioned Dan.

"The best way to understand the resolution stage is to..."

"Experience it," jumped in Dan.

"Right on," said the One Minute Manager.

"Let me see. This stage is often fairly brief," thought the One Minute Manager.

Suddenly the intercom on the One Minute Manager's desk came alive. "Louise Gilmore is on the line. Should I have her call later?"

"Wait a moment," replied the One Minute Manager. "I'll take it now." Turning to Dan with a smile, he said, "Excuse the interruption, Dan, but this may be exactly what we are looking for."

"Hello, Louise. What can I do you for?"

After a long silence, the One Minute Manager smiled broadly. "That's wonderful, Louise. As I've said, you have to trust the process. It works. By the way, how would you feel about a visitor in your meeting tomorrow morning? He is a friend of mine who is interested in how groups develop and it sounds like your meeting would fill a missing gap. Thanks. He will be there."

"It's all set. Tomorrow you will attend a strategic planning meeting that Louise is running—that is, if you'd care to."

"Of course," Dan responded eagerly.

The next morning Dan arrived early at the office. He had spent the cab ride thinking of how fortunate he was to have met such a special person who seemed to get real pleasure in sharing information with others. Information is power and the One Minute Manager gave it freely.

Louise Gilmore, the vice president of strategic planning, was sitting quietly at her desk when Dan arrived. She seemed to come alive when he walked in and with a big smile and firm handshake greeted him warmly. Dan was struck by her vitality and friendliness.

Together they entered the meeting room where the six group members were chatting and joking amicably.

Louise introduced Dan as he found a seat. All team members greeted him cordially but with a bit of reserve. Dan couldn't help feeling that his presence made them a bit uncomfortable.

The meeting began with Louise reviewing the struggle the group had had in determining next year's direction and goals and then the outcomes they had finally agreed upon. There was much joking and laughing during the review and friendly kidding of one another. It seemed that they enjoyed and valued each other's company in spite of or because of the prior disagreements Louise had mentioned. Louise laughed along with them.

Today's agenda began with new decisions to be made. The group engaged immediately, listening to one another, building on each other's ideas and often agreeing readily. Dan watched in fascination at how smoothly things were proceeding. After opening the meeting, Louise gave control of the meeting to other members as the topics of discussion changed.

There was an air of respect and politeness in the group. Dan noticed some members became less vocal as time went on. Much to his surprise, just as Dan assumed a decision was made, Louise spoke up.

"Bill, you haven't said anything for the past ten minutes. Are you having some reservations?"

"Well, yes, but they are minor," replied Bill.

"Please share them," said Louise. "If you remember, our best, most creative decisions have come from our disagreements."

"OK," replied Bill and he proceeded cautiously. At first the others protested and then the group began a heated discussion of the pros and cons of the new points Bill had made.

Dan thought to himself, "Uh, oh, she's lost it. The group had been working well before this."

Louise listened, facilitated disagreements, built on the merits of each position and added her own. Others began to do likewise.

Somewhat tentatively Bill spoke up again. "Building on the plans on which we've agreed, if our expected profit in new products is solid and the cuts we're making in other departments are adequate, we could afford to invest in needed capital improvements."

As he spoke, others listened and heads began to nod. Bill then asked if there was a consensus on the decision. All group members responded enthusiastically. Shortly after, the meeting adjourned. There was a feeling of accomplishment and eagerness in the air.

The group members sauntered out, each stopping to shake hands with Dan. Group members seemed to feel confident and productive. Dan heard comments like: "Good meeting." "Glad you could join us," and, "We got through that one."

When the room emptied, Louise and the One Minute Manager joined him. "Well Dan, what did you think?"

"Amazing," replied Dan. "I thought the group had blown it for a while, but individuals seemed to feel better and more confident after they had disagreed. Also, I noticed you opened the meeting, then let them manage it, but you jumped back in and helped them out as necessary."

"You've got it," smiled Louise. "People are feeling good because they have worked through some struggles together. It's like in a new marriage when neither spouse wants to disagree even when they don't agree. Later after they work through some differences, their marriage can be stronger. The danger to a group occurs when this euphoric feeling prevents a loss of productivity that comes from disagreement. The result can be a tendency toward Groupthink."

"Groupthink, what's that?" interrupted Dan.

"A famous psychologist coined that term," replied the One Minute Manager, "while studying some groups that were advising the presidents of the United States. Irving Janis discovered that, often, social pressure prevented members from disagreeing."

"Oh, so Groupthink occurs when group members are afraid to disagree so they don't say anything at all," responded Dan thoughtfully. "No one is willing to rock the boat."

"Exactly. My role at this point is to encourage disagreement and to help the team work through the conflict. I'm concerned about the group developing the confidence to manage disagreement and to value differences. These are all important activities in the *Resolution* Stage—the stage this group is in."

"In addition, the group was beginning to manage itself. If I continue to be in there directing, however, that would never happen. My role at this stage is to support their efforts at self-management and to model effective membership."

"But what if they really get into trouble?" questioned Dan.

"Rest assured, I'd be there," replied Louise with a smile.

"I'm sure you would," said Dan. "And thank you. You've helped me a lot."

"Don't mention it," said Louise as she handed Dan a card. 'You-know-who' wanted me to give you this card which describes Stage 3: Resolution:"

Group Development Stage 3—Resolution

Characteristics

- Decreasing dissatisfaction
- Resolving discrepancies between expectations and reality
- Resolving polarities and animosities
- Developing harmony, trust, support and respect
- Developing self-esteem and confidence
- Being more open and giving more feedback
- Sharing responsibility and control
- Using team language

"What are the big-picture learnings from your visits to some of our work teams?" asked the One Minute Manager as Dan Brockway entered his office.

"First of all, there are four different stages of group development that a team can be in at any one moment in time," said Dan. "The first stage for most groups is *orientation* where *productivity* is *low* because group members are not clear on goals and tasks and have minimal knowledge and skills about how to function as a team. *Morale* is *high*, though, as everyone is excited about being a part of the group and has high expectations.

At the other extreme is *production* where the team is humming. *Productivity* is *high* as group members have the knowledge, skills and *morale* to be a *high*-performing team. In between those two extremes are two stages: *dissatisfaction*, when the honeymoon is over and the initial high expectations of the group are seen as being more difficult to achieve; and *resolution*, when the group is learning to work together resolving differences and developing confidence and cohesion."

"Good summary," said the One Minute Manager. "Any other learnings?"

"I noticed that productivity increased slowly through the four stages," said Dan. "It started low in orientation, and continued to improve through dissatisfaction and resolution until it was high in production. On the other hand, morale or enthusiasm started high in orientation and then took a dip in dissatisfaction, but then it began to increase again in resolution and production."

"I'm impressed that you noticed that," said the One Minute Manager. "One group development theorist has put those dimensions on a chart that shows how morale and productivity vary during each stage. It looks something like this," he said as he drew the chart on the flipchart.

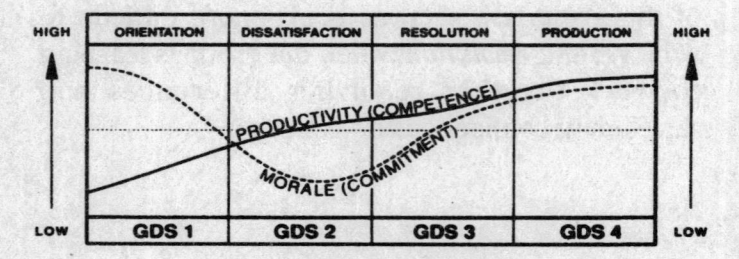

	ORIENTATION	DISSATISFACTION	RESOLUTION	PRODUCTION	
HIGH			PRODUCTIVITY (COMPETENCE)		HIGH
			MORALE (COMMITMENT)		
LOW	GDS 1	GDS 2	GDS 3	GDS 4	LOW

GROUP DEVELOPMENT STAGES

*Adapted from R.B. Lacoursiere, *The Life Cycle of Groups: Group Developmental Stage Theory* (New York: Human Service Press, 1980).

"The GDS stands for 'Group Development Stage.' Notice how the productivity and morale dimensions change," said the One Minute Manager.

"That's very helpful," said Dan. "It makes it seem very clear."

"Pictures are often worth a thousand words. Any other insights?"

"Yes," said Dan. "It seems each stage needs a different type of leadership. Here's where I want more information. How does a group leader know the very best way to work with a team during each stage?"

"**I**T sounds like you have mastered diagnosis and now you are ready to learn adaptability—when to use what leadership style. That requires that you become a *Situational Leader*," smiled the One Minute Manager.

"A what?"

"A Situational Leader," repeated the One Minute Manager. "For a long time it was thought that there were only two ways to manage a team of people: autocratically or democratically. With autocratic leadership the emphasis was on telling your people what to do, how to do it, where to do it, and when to do it. Group performance was paramount. With democratic leadership the emphasis was on listening to your people, praising their efforts and facilitating their interactions with each other. Group morale was deemed to be the best way to maximize the group's performance. There were two problems with these two extremes of leadership."

"I bet one of them was the either/or way of looking at things," interjected Dan. "That always leads to an 'I'm right, you're wrong' way of looking at the world."

"Precisely," said the One Minute Manager. "As a result, we would have great pendulum swings in terms of managing groups. If you were too autocratic, people would complain after a while and say: 'You're too tough. You're stifling creativity,' and, 'You're controlling everything.' Then, feeling bad, the leader would shift over to the other extreme and involve everyone in decision making with a more democratic and participative leadership style."

"But that could be overused as well, right?" asked Dan.

"Absolutely," said the One Minute Manager. "And then pretty soon everyone would be complaining that people are feeling good but nothing is getting done. There is too much socializing, or meetings are taking too long."

"And pretty soon there would be another drastic shift to the other extreme," laughed Dan. "A real yo-yo. I've certainly seen that."

"You've got it," said the One Minute Manager. "What I like about Situational Leadership is that it eliminates that flip-flop approach while, at the same time, recognizes that there are two behaviors involved in leadership: directive or autocratic behavior, and supportive or democratic behavior." With that, the One Minute Manager began to draw a large square and divide it into four equal boxes. When he finished labeling the boxes, he handed it to Dan:

THE FOUR LEADERSHIP STYLES OF SITUATIONAL LEADERSHIP ® II

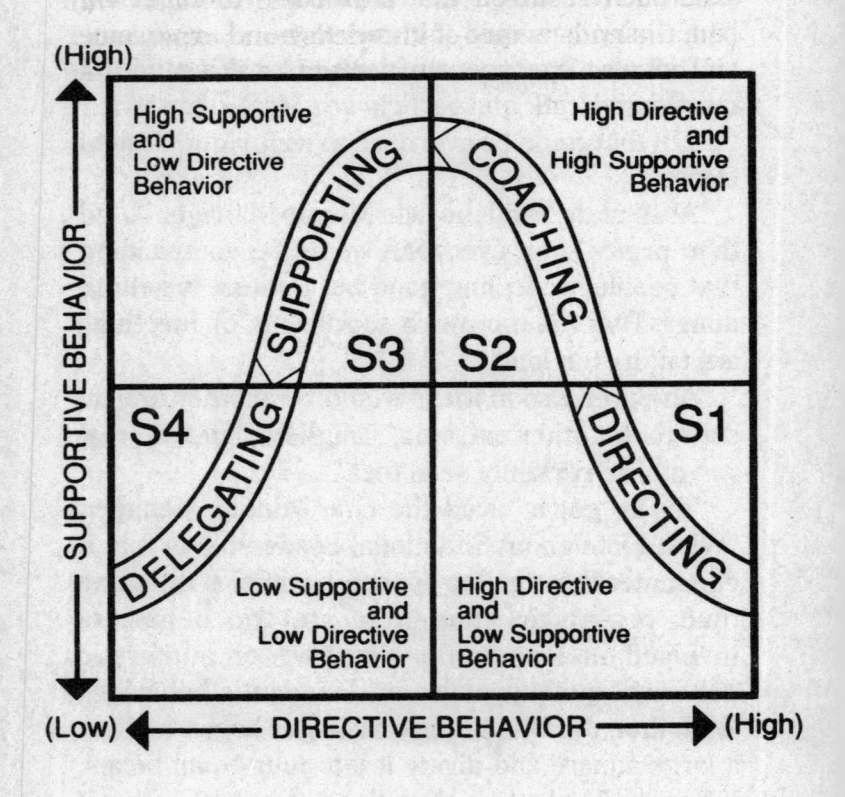

	(High)	
SUPPORTIVE BEHAVIOR	High Supportive and Low Directive Behavior — **SUPPORTING** — S3	High Directive and High Supportive Behavior — **COACHING** — S2
	S4 — **DELEGATING** — Low Supportive and Low Directive Behavior	S1 — **DIRECTING** — High Directive and Low Supportive Behavior
(Low)	← DIRECTIVE BEHAVIOR →	(High)

"I used to be a school teacher when I first got out of college," continued the One Minute Manager when Dan looked up from examining the drawing. "There were two different approaches to teaching depending on your assumptions about kids. One approach assumed that kids come to class with their barrels empty of knowledge and experience. If that was the case, what would be the job of the teacher?"

"To fill up their barrels with knowledge," smiled Dan.

"Exactly," said the One Minute Manager. "To me, directing is a barrel-filling style. That's exactly what is needed when a group is in the orientation stage of development. People are confused about roles and goals and there is a high need for information and skills. The reason a lot of supportive behavior is not needed in this stage is that group members are already enthusiastic and committed."

"That's the style that Ron Tilman used with his new task force and it seemed appropriate."

"It was," said the One Minute Manager. "If Ron had started with being participative and supportive, it would have been inappropriate because the task force came to its first meeting needing information and direction. Their barrels were *empty*."

"When is it more important to be supporting then?" asked Dan.

"When the group already has experience and skills working together but for some reason has become bogged down. In our teaching analogy, the second approach assumed that students bring to class a *'full* barrel' of knowledge and experience but it is not particularly organized. Therefore, it's the job of the teacher to draw that knowledge and experience out of the kids and then help them organize it. Supporting is a "barrel drawing-out" activity. The leader listens, supports, and facilitates the group's interactions."

"That's what Louise Gilmore did with the strategic planning committee," said Dan. "She drew almost everything from the group."

"That was appropriate for that committee," said the One Minute Manager. "They had moved past the Dissatisfaction Stage and were learning to work with each other. They didn't need a lot of direction because they had developed the skills necessary to function as a team."

"How do the skills of coaching and delegating fit into this?"

"Coaching is high on both directive behavior and supportive behavior and delegating is low on both behaviors," said the One Minute Manager.

"Is coaching, then, a "barrel-filling" and "barrel drawing-out" activity?"

"Yes, indeed," said the One Minute Manager. "It involves directing and supporting, telling and listening."

"Susan Schaefer used that style with her productivity improvement group. Since they were dissatisfied, morale was dropping and they needed to express their opinions and they needed support from her."

"But since they were still developing skills as a group," said the One Minute Manager, "they also required direction."

"With a delegating style like Neil used with the shipping department," said Dan, "neither "barrel filling" nor "barrel drawing-out" is needed because the group's barrel is not only filled, but it is organized."

"You have that right," said the One Minute Manager. "Now you can see why adaptability is important."

Dan leaned back in a reflective way and said, "It seems like...

*

EFFECTIVE

TEAM LEADERS

ADJUST THEIR STYLE

TO PROVIDE

WHAT THE GROUP

CAN'T PROVIDE

FOR ITSELF

*

"**THAT'S** a good way to put it," said the One Minute Manager. "For any group to be effective, someone has to be attending to both task functions and maintenance functions. The question is whether it has to be the designated group leader or not."

"Task functions?" wondered Dan.

"*Task functions* are behaviors which focus on getting the job done," said the One Minute Manager. "They focus on what the group is supposed to be doing. Task functions include activities such as setting the agenda, establishing goals, giving direction, initiating discussion, setting time limits, giving and seeking information and summarizing."

"So task functions are related to directive behavior," said Dan. "What are maintenance functions?"

"Group *maintenance functions* focus on developing and maintaining the group's harmony and cohesiveness. Such activities focus on how the group is functioning. They include recognition, listening, encouraging participation, conflict management and relationship building."

"Those are all supportive behaviors?"

"They sure are," said the One Minute Manager. "What you need to learn, and Situational Leadership® certainly helps, is that, although these functions need to be fulfilled for a group to be effective, filling them is not necessarily the job of the manager or designated team leader. In fact, as group members are able to take over these functions, it is best for the manager to move out of those roles."

"So there is a smooth transition of leadership style and functions as the group progresses," said Dan.

"That's exactly right," said the One Minute Manager.

"In the Orientation Stage, group members bring enthusiasm and commitment to meetings, but little knowledge, so they need direction (Directing-S1). In the Dissatisfaction Stage, group members are not high on either competence or commitment. They are struggling with the task as well as how to work together so they need both direction and support (Coaching-S2). In the Resolution Stage, group members have the skills to perform well but still need to build their confidence or morale so they need support and encouragement (Supporting-S3). And finally, when a group reaches the Production Stage they have high skills and morale so the leader can stand aside or join in and let them work with minimal interference (Delegating-S4)."

"So in the Orientation Stage, task functions are the main concern for the leader," said Dan. "While in the Dissatisfaction Stage, the group is not able to handle either task or maintenance concerns. As a result, the burden for both falls on the leader. In the Resolution Stage, the group is managing the task concerns but needs help on group maintenance. Then, finally, in the Production Stage both task and maintenance functions are being attended to by group members.

"It sounds as if you have a good grasp of those concepts," said the One Minute Manager.

"Yes," said Dan, "I'm excited about how all this fits together and I can't wait to get back to Maria Sanchez and tell her what I've learned."

"That's a good idea," said the One Minute Manager. "I find that one of the best ways to test my own understanding is to try to teach someone else."

"Great," said Dan. "I think I'll call her as soon as I get back to the office and arrange a lunch meeting."

"Listen," said the One Minute Manager, "I'd like to meet Maria. Would you mind if I joined you and sat back while you share those ideas?"

"That would be perfect," Dan replied. " It would be a good check for me and since you've convinced me how perceptive Maria is, she might come up with some questions I haven't thought of. Let's call her right now and set the time."

That Friday, Dan, Maria and the One Minute Manager met for lunch. After ordering their meal, Dan pulled out a folder from his briefcase and began.

"Maria," he said, "that letter you wrote about teamwork was really unsettling to me so I called my friend, the One Minute Manager for some help. I wanted some advice about how to convince you that what we were teaching was right. To my surprise, he agreed with your comments about the importance of working in groups. He's been showing me how working in groups differs from managing one-on-one. I've been spending some time observing groups in action and talking with the One Minute Manager concerning his ideas about team development and leadership. I wanted to share with you what I've learned, so I put this Situational Leadership® II diagram together that, I think, summarizes how a leader can best work with and develop a group into a high-performing team." Dan pulled the diagram out of his folder and explained the stages of group development, told Maria how each called for different leadership behaviors, and described the changes in productivity and morale that occurred over time.

SITUATIONAL LEADERSHIP® II

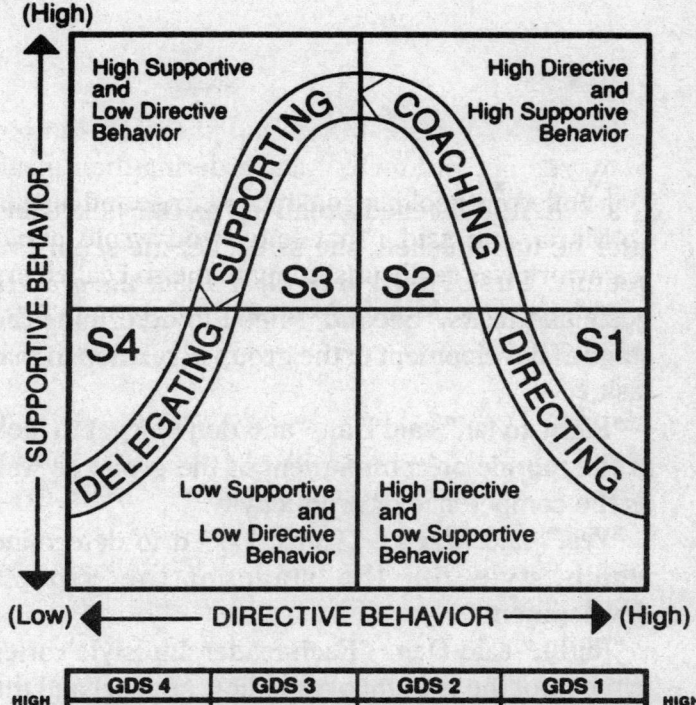

SUPPORTIVE BEHAVIOR (Low → High)
DIRECTIVE BEHAVIOR (Low → High)

- **S3 – SUPPORTING**: High Supportive and Low Directive Behavior
- **S2 – COACHING**: High Directive and High Supportive Behavior
- **S4 – DELEGATING**: Low Supportive and Low Directive Behavior
- **S1 – DIRECTING**: High Directive and Low Supportive Behavior

GDS 4	GDS 3	GDS 2	GDS 1
PRODUCTION	RESOLUTION	DISSATISFACTION	ORIENTATION

PRODUCTIVITY (COMPETENCE)
MORALE (COMMITMENT)

*Adapted from R.B. Lacoursiere, *The Life Cycle of Groups: Group Developmental Stage Theory* (New York: Human Service Press. 1980).

MATCHING LEADERSHIP STYLE TO STAGE OF GROUP DEVELOPMENT

MARIA listened attentively as Dan talked and after he had finished, she said, "Let me see if I've got this. First, I need to be clear about the group's goals and tasks. Second, I need to determine the stage of development of the group in relation to that task."

"Right so far," said Dan, "and don't forget to look at the morale or commitment of the group as well as the competence or productivity."

"Yes," said Maria. "Third, I need to determine which style fits the stage of the group's development."

"Right," said Dan. "Each leadership style varies in terms of the amount of direction, support and the involvement of the group in making decisions. In S1 the leader is primarily responsible for direction setting. In S4 the group sets direction and makes decisions."

"I think I understand, Dan," said Maria. "It seems clear and straightforward and I think it fits some of the groups I am working with. I'd like to try some of your thoughts out and see how they work for me. Do you think we could meet again in two weeks to discuss these ideas after I've had a chance to use them?"

At that, the One Minute Manager jumped in and said, "I think that's an excellent idea. After you have tested the ideas, you may have some additional thoughts and questions. I would look forward to that discussion."

"I would too," said Dan. "Maria, I'm glad you wrote that letter. I certainly have learned a lot from all this and I'm going to do some more thinking also. Let's all get together the week after next, same time, same place."

During the next two weeks Maria focused primarily on two groups. The first was a quality task force that had just recently been convened and it was easy to diagnose that they were in the Orientation Stage. They were not clear about goals and hadn't yet defined their individual roles or an action plan. Maria decided to focus the group's energy on understanding goals, establishing roles and defining the skills needed and the necessary first steps. The meeting went well and Maria felt good about the progress made.

The other group was Maria's own work unit. It was harder for her to diagnose the stage this group was in. They seemed to like, enjoy and support each other, but there was an underlying uneasiness and some tension between some of the members of the group. She couldn't decide whether they were in the Dissatisfaction or Resolution Stage and so she had more difficulty in deciding what leadership style would work best. Maria wasn't sure if her close connection with her group might be distorting her views. As she reflected on her work in preparation for the meeting with Dan and the One Minute Manager, she jotted down several questions in her notebook:

1. Can a group move from Orientation to Production without the help of a team leader?
2. Once I determine a group's developmental stage and have decided on a leadership style, how long should I stay with that leadership style?
3. Can a manager's involvement with the unit get in the way of her ability to diagnose its stage of development?

When Maria, Dan and the One Minute Manager got together, Maria immediately spoke up. "I'm glad to see you both," she said. "I've had some success with using the model but it has raised some questions for me as well. I've written my questions down on this sheet of paper." Dan and the One Minute Manager read over the list. "These are very important concerns," said the One Minute Manager. "I think we should take them in order."

"Wait a minute," said Dan, "I'd like to add one other question to the list. One of the units in my plant has been functioning beautifully for six months, but last week when I was there they seemed to be very tentative in their behavior, reluctant to speak out, and I felt some unspoken tension. It didn't seem like the same team I'd met with last month so my question is: 'Do teams ever regress to a previous developmental stage? If so, why, and what can be done to prevent it?' "

"That's quite a set of questions," said the One Minute Manager. "Let's finish our lunch and go over to the office. I think we could work better with a flipchart and room to spread out our work."

Back in the office as Maria put the four questions on a flipchart, the One Minute Manager got a poster from his conference room and taped it on the wall.

*

THE MOST IMPORTANT

FUNCTION

OF A TEAM LEADER

IS TO HELP

THE GROUP

MOVE THROUGH THE

STAGES OF DEVELOPMENT

*

THE One Minute Manager explained, "I put this statement up because I think it relates to your first question, Maria."

"I take it from that," Maria said, "that diagnosing the stage of development and being adaptable enough to deliver the appropriate leadership style are the first two skills, but they are just the beginning. My primary job is to continue to change my style whenever possible to help the group move through the stages to Stage 4 where they will be a high-performing team."

"That's it," replied the One Minute Manager. "Now we're talking about the third skill—empowerment—that an effective group leader needs to develop besides diagnosis and adaptability. Empowerment involves gradually turning over the responsibility for direction and support to the group. It's managing the journey from dependence on the leader to interdependence, from external control to internal control. I can illustrate this best by referring back to the four basic Situational Leadership® II styles." With that, the One Minute Manager quickly drew the model on a second flipchart he had in front of the room.

SITUATIONAL LEADERSHIP® II

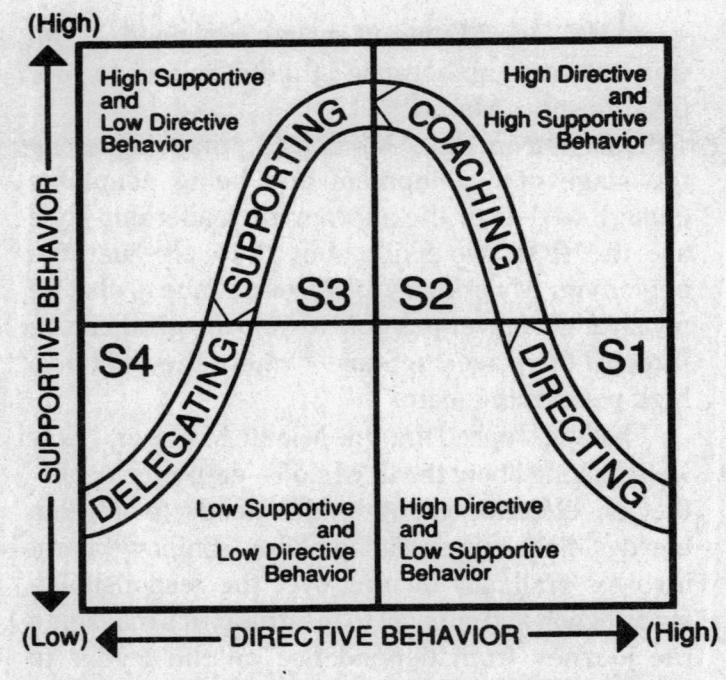

(High)

SUPPORTIVE BEHAVIOR

S3 — SUPPORTING
High Supportive and Low Directive Behavior

S2 — COACHING
High Directive and High Supportive Behavior

S4 — DELEGATING
Low Supportive and Low Directive Behavior

S1 — DIRECTING
High Directive and Low Supportive Behavior

(Low) ← DIRECTIVE BEHAVIOR → **(High)**

*Adapted from R.B. Lacoursiere, *The Life Cycle of Groups: Group Developmental Stage Theory* (New York: Human Service Press. 1980).

FOUR BASIC LEADERSHIP STYLES

"Imagine the curve going through the leadership styles is a railroad track. If you want to get from Style 1 to Style 4, what two stations do you have to stop at along the way?"

"Style 2–Coaching and Style 3–Supporting," said Dan. "If that's true, then I would assume it's not possible to skip a stage. In other words, you couldn't go right from Orientation to Production."

"Except for some groups that might start in Stage 2 as we discussed earlier, groups generally do not skip stages. No matter how sophisticated team members are about the task or how experienced they are in group dynamics, they still have to create a team and the process of developing a high performing team requires going through those states. That also means that your leadership style has to follow this same track—you can't skip a style."

"That's really interesting," said Maria. "In retrospect I can remember several times when I've started off using a supportive (S3), participative style with a new group, particularly when the group was set up as a quality circle or employee problem-solving group.

"How did it work?"

"Horribly," said Maria. "I drove them immediately into dissatisfaction. Then, not knowing what I was doing, I would get angry and move straight from a supporting Style 3 to a directing Style 1. And that really made the group more angry and more unhappy."

"My rule of thumb," said the One Minute Manager," is when in doubt, whether it be a new group or an already established group, start with a more directive style because if you have misdiagnosed and the group is farther along in its developmental stage than you thought, it is much easier to loosen up than tighten up. But if you assume a group is further along than it is and you start off too participative and supportive and you have to back up and be more directive, members will resent it, even if it is appropriate."

"So you're saying people in general resent tightening up on leadership style," said Maria.

"Absolutely," said the One Minute Manager. "I used to tell my wife when she was a teacher not to smile too much until November. If she started off as Ms. Human Relations and wanted to be the kids' friend right away and they did not perform, it would be murder to retain control."

"I think I buy this managing the journey role for team leaders and recognize the importance of staying on the railroad tracks," said Maria. "But I could use some help on my second question—how long should you stay at each station?"

"REMEMBER our discussion a couple of weeks ago," said the One Minute Manager, "when we said that a directing style is for the Orientation Stage. It's a start-up style and should be used to share necessary information, explain initial goals and tasks and help the group develop the skills necessary to become more effective. If a manager stays in a highly directive style for long, however, team members will soon feel resentment about being told over and over what to do and how to do it. They will be less inclined to contribute their ideas and opinions. Productivity, satisfaction, and creativity will all suffer as a result."

"That makes a lot of sense to me," said Maria. "I know that whenever I have been in that kind of a group situation I don't feel I have much personal influence and thus soon lose interest."

"That's right," said the One Minute Manager. "And that's why it's important to move very quickly to a coaching style and to begin to encourage members to share their ideas and opinions. People begin to feel empowered when their ideas are valued. Remember, a group can have process goals such as open communication and shared leadership as well as task goals. Stating those goals is often a good way to move to a coaching style and to encourage input from team members."

"Good idea," said Maria. "But why do groups move into a stage of dissatisfaction if the leadership behavior has shifted to coaching at an appropriate time?"

"That's a good question," said the One Minute Manager. "It would be nice to avoid that dissatisfaction stage and move to being a high-performing team. Appropriate leadership behavior at the right time can certainly reduce the amount of dissatisfaction, but it will never eliminate it. As people begin to express their opinions and state their needs, differences will emerge. As a result, some members get competitive with one another and engage in power struggles, others withdraw and still others get discouraged and frustrated with the difficulty of the task. The reality of the hard work sets in after the honeymoon is over. The team is struggling during the Dissatisfaction Stage for a sense of purpose and independence. It's a time of turbulence."

"Yes. It sounds like something to avoid if possible," said Maria.

"Not so!" said the One Minute Manager. "It's a creative and dynamic stage as well. As I mentioned to Dan, it is the adolescent stage in a group's life. The group has to go through this awkward period before it can move to adulthood and the Production Stage. Unfortunately, lots of groups get stuck in this stage and that's what leads to the negative feelings about groups that is so common. I have found that just knowing that this stage is inevitable helps me keep my commitment to persevere and to progress to the next stage."

"What is needed at this point," continued the One Minute Manager, "is to gradually reduce the amount of direction and to increase the encouragement and support the manager gives. Morale is declining and so we need to find ways to catch the team doing things right as well as to continue to help build skills and knowledge. The team needs to learn how to manage their communication and decision making. It needs to develop ground rules for listening and managing conflict and encouraging everyone's input. Remember, we need to try to provide the kind of behavior that the team is not able to provide for itself."

Dan jumped in at this point and said, "What you just said turned on a light for me. You don't just jump from a directing to a coaching style. You gradually reduce the amount of direction or task behavior and increase the amount of support or process behavior as you progress through each stage."

"You've got it," said the One Minute Manager. "It's a step-by-step process. Don't forget, in addition to increasing support and reducing direction you're also increasing team involvement in the decision-making process. This by itself is a supportive behavior, an empowering behavior. Team responsibility for both the task and the process is increasing and consequently the team should become less dependent on the formal leader."

"What happens if this process continues?" asked Dan. "Does the group leader work himself right out of a job?"

"Well, not quite," said the One Minute Manager. "There's always a role for a team leader, but it doesn't mean maintaining control or keeping the team dependent upon the leader. In fact:

*YOU WILL
NEVER, NEVER, NEVER
HAVE
AN EMPOWERED,
SELF-DIRECTED TEAM
UNLESS THE MANAGER
IS WILLING
TO SHARE CONTROL*

"If we're interested in productivity and human satisfaction," continued the One Minute Manager, "it is important that everyone involved be empowered to influence the decisions that affect them."

"It may go beyond productivity and satisfaction," said Maria thoughtfully. "I read an article the other day that suggests that people who are involved in decisions at work actually live longer than those who are not."

"Interesting," said the One Minute Manager, "and it makes sense. I know that the most devastating situations in my career are those times when I have no say in important decisions that affect me at work."

"Well, getting back to group development and changing leadership behavior," said Maria, "the leader has to gradually give up control in order for the group to become successful and self-directed."

"Not quite give it up," said the One Minute Manager, "but rather be willing to share it. When that happens the leader is no longer making decisions for the group, but rather participating in these decisions. The group with the leader as a member is now a self-directed team"

"That's a tough shift for a lot of us," said Dan, "because as a manager I've been taught that making decisions and maintaining control is my job."

"I know," said the One Minute Manager, "and what I am suggesting is that your job as a manager is to help people and teams develop so they have competence and commitment and the ability to share in making decisions. Remember, a high-performing team is more creative and better at problem solving than any individual functioning alone."

"I think you have answered my first two questions about the role of the team leader and how long one should stay in a particular leadership style," said Maria. "It would seem to me to be more appropriate to discuss Dan's question around regression before we move to my concerns about diagnosis and involvement."

"Sounds fine to me," said the One Minute Manager. "Fire away, Dan."

"Once groups are in the Production Stage, do they ever regress?" asked Dan.

"Yes, they do," replied the One Minute Manager. "When groups gain, lose or change members, when the task changes or if a major event occurs which disrupts group functioning, the group will move back to Stage 3 and even into Stage 2. You can expect it."

"As a leader, then, you need to move your leadership to match the stage," said Dan.

"Right you are," said the One Minute Manager. "When you are dealing with a high-performing team and you are delegating, if a problem occurs, you can't go from Delegating (Style 4), back to Directing (Style 1). That would be the ultimate derailment. You have to back track to Supporting (Style 3) and try to find out what's going wrong. Then you determine whether you need to move back to Coaching (Style 2) and either redirect or reprimand to get the group back to proper functioning."

"So when a setback occurs," said Dan, "you're suggesting I need to keep on the railroad tracks and move back one leadership style at a time until I can get the group to deal with the problem."

"You've got it," said the One Minute Manager. "Just be careful not to get derailed by jumping the track and skipping a style forward to reinforce growth in group development or backward to handle a regression.

"That's helpful," said Dan. "I think I need to hear that over and over again. Let's go to Maria's last question. Can a manager get so involved that he or she can't decide what stage a group is in? I'm particularly interested in that question because it involves the team leader's role of participant observer."

"What?" wondered Maria.

"Before I began observing some of the work groups in the One Minute Manager's company he told me that an effective team leader had to be fully engaged in the *content* or agenda — what the group was working on — and yet be able to step back and observe the *process* or dynamics which are occuring.

"That's exactly what I'm talking about," said Maria. "Sometimes I felt I was so emotionally involved in the decision itself, it was hard to be aware of how the decision was being made and therefore what stage of development the group was in."

"When I was observing your groups," said Dan, turning to the One Minute Manager, "I didn't have that problem because I wasn't actually a member of the group. I was just a *process observer*."

"Good point," said the One Minute Manager. "One strategy I often use to minimize the impact my involvement may have on the clarity of my observation is to assign a group member to be the process observer for the group and report periodically on what he or she has observed about communication, decision making, conflict management or other areas of concern. While that member is playing that role, he or she cannot get involved in the content of the discussion."

"Why not?" asked Maria.

"It helps in the beginning when members are learning observation skills to separate out the two roles. However, if at any time in the discussion the process observer feels strongly about what is being discussed, that person can ask to be relieved of the process role so he or she can get involved in the content. Someone else will then step out and assume the role."

"That sounds interesting," said Maria. "So you rotate the process consultant role."

"Yes," said the One Minute Manager. "This helps teach the skills of process observation to all of the group members and raises the awareness of the group about how it is functioning."

"Then if there is a problem or we get stuck, we can use the process information to help us understand what the problems are so we can do something about them. Being fully aware of our own behavior helps move the group through its developmental stages."

"Could you explain that in more detail?" Maria interjected.

"I had a group one time in the Dissatisfaction Stage. I was so embroiled in it, I was helpless. I knew we were in trouble, but I didn't know why or what to do about it. I couldn't tell if we were in Stage 1 or 2," said the One Minute Manager.

"Shouldn't that difference have been clear?" asked Maria somewhat surprised.

"No, not really. Energy was very high and tension was obvious. However questions were about roles and goals and strategies which I thought were orientation needs. Nothing fit neatly."

"Go on," said Maria.

"Well, on a whim, you see I was very new at this, I asked one group member to sit outside the group for one hour and observe how we were communicating. I provided her with a list of questions to serve as a guide like: Who talks? Who talks to whom? Who follows whom? At the end of the hour she reported back. Much to our dismay she counted forty times in that one hour when we interrupted one another."

"Just that one piece of information helped us identify a real problem characteristic of the Dissatisfaction Stage and correct it. All group members monitored their own interactions and we made great strides toward resolution," continued the One Minute Manager.

"I see," said Maria. "You could also give the list to all members to fill out periodically during a meeting to monitor your progress, couldn't you?"

"Yes. A strategy such as that promotes both awareness and mutual responsibility to monitor group functioning," smiled the One Minute Manager.

"How about using a third party to sit in your meeting and monitor group process?" asked Dan, who had been sitting quietly. "That way you wouldn't have to pull a member out or take meeting time to focus on process issues."

"That is also a strategy and a useful one, especially if the group is stuck. Sometimes a third, uninvolved party can give straight objective feedback which a member could not do. It could be just the stimulation the group needs. In those cases the process observer acts as an objective candid camera which removes any question of vested interest," said the One Minute Manager.

"I can see how that could be very helpful in the Dissatisfaction Stage or whenever you want objective help with team building from an outside source," agreed Maria.

"Yes. It can be very helpful to the group," said the One Minute Manager, "but I wouldn't depend on it as a steady diet. Remember, the important thing is to transfer the skills of participant observation to the group. Group members need to assume the responsibility of their own monitoring or they will never become a high-performing team. Your job as a one minute manager is to *empower* them."

"I can see how that is essential," said Dan. "Groups are so complex there is no way I could stay on top of all that's going on myself.

THE One Minute Manager sat back quietly for a moment. A pensive look came over his face. Then he spoke. "Years ago my mentor taught me a powerful lesson about empowerment. One day I was complaining about how overloaded I felt. I was responsible for all that went on in my department and couldn't keep up. He listened patiently while I ranted and raved and then said simply, 'You're missing the point. Your job is to educate your people, to help them develop to the point where they can take responsibility for their work and to give them opportunities to perform.' I was taken aback. Seeing this, he went on to explain:

*

THE WORDS "MANAGER" AND "EDUCATOR" ARE SYNONYMOUS

*

"Don't you mean trainer rather than educator?" asked Dan.

"No," said the One Minute Manager. "You have to remember that we train animals but we educate teams. As a manager you are a teacher. Your primary job is to develop your people. You can't depend on seminars or training sessions to do that for you. In every group there is a well of creativity and talent. Your job is to help all team members develop the skills and knowledge so they become self-directed *and* to provide an environment where they feel willing to risk, to grow, to take responsibility and to use their creativity. Unless you do this, you will constantly feel behind the eight ball and what's worse, you will never be involved with self-directed teams. It's a self-fulfilling prophecy. If you believe groups can be high performing and you help them develop the appropriate skills and knowledge and the freedom to act, teams will respond both creatively and responsibly. That will make your life a whole lot easier."

"So empowering means helping teams develop their skills and knowledge and supporting them to use their talents," replied Maria.

"That's right," agreed the One Minute Manager. "An important thing to remember is that to be fully contributing, individuals and groups have to feel free to do so. In fact, they have to know that you want them to win. When they know that, groups will strive to be the best. They will set stretching goals, assume responsibility and take risks. Even critical feedback will be accepted if groups see it as part of their developmental process and if it is focused on helping them win."

"That's powerful stuff," exclaimed Maria.

"That's empowerment," smiled the One Minute Manager. "Teams feel empowered when they are involved, contributing and productive."

"Well I've felt involved, contributing and productive working with you both," said Dan. "This has been a very important meeting for me. Both of you have been so helpful."

"Learning from each other is what it's all about," replied the One Minute Manager checking his watch. "Real empowerment comes from sharing. I don't mean just with each other, but with members on every team. I have a board meeting in half an hour so I'll need to move along. It's been a pleasure meeting with you, Maria, and thank you for your letter that started the ball rolling. If I can be of further assistance call me anytime. Good luck."

"Thanks," said Maria. "I will. I'm going to use my own work unit as a focus for these concepts."

"I'm anxious to continue to use what I've learned, too," said Dan.

Almost immediately both Dan and Maria began applying what they had learned from the One Minute Manager about group leadership. In fact, Dan integrated the concepts in the Essentials of Management course he was teaching.

He taught the managers in the program that the steps to empowering others begin with *diagnosis*. In determining the stage of development he suggested that they might use the characteristics of high-performing teams as an initial comparison. Everyone learned to use the acronym PERFORM.

Once the stage of development is determined, Dan told the managers, the second step would be to *determine the appropriate leadership style* needed based on the amount of directive and supportive behavior and the group's involvement in decision-making. And then, finally, *specific strategies* to help the group in its development had to be determined, like clarifying roles and goals if they were unclear or teaching conflict resolution or appointing a process consultant if team members' opinions were becoming polarized.

Once specific needs have been determined Dan advised the managers to develop a specific *action plan for managing the journey* to group empowerment.

Dan created a pocket size "Game Plan" to make it easier for the managers he taught to become effective team leaders.

TEAM DEVELOPMENT GAME PLAN

1. **Determine Vision**
   Set Goals and Roles

   Then

2. **Diagnosis**

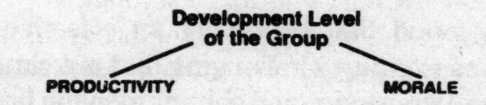

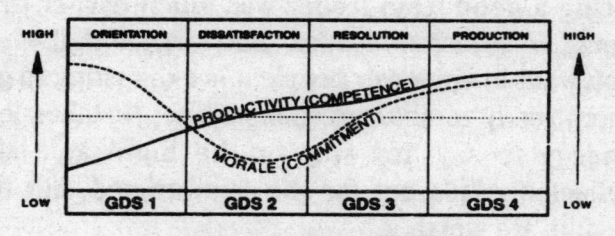

   Development Level of the Group

   PRODUCTIVITY ———— MORALE

HIGH	ORIENTATION	DISSATISFACTION	RESOLUTION	PRODUCTION	HIGH
LOW	GDS 1	GDS 2	GDS 3	GDS 4	LOW

   PRODUCTIVITY (COMPETENCE)
   MORALE (COMMITMENT)

   GROUP DEVELOPMENT STAGES

   Then

3. **Match Appropriate Leadership Style**

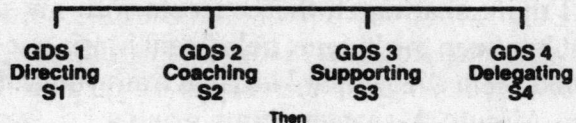

GDS 1	GDS 2	GDS 3	GDS 4
Directing	Coaching	Supporting	Delegating
S1	S2	S3	S4

   Then

4. **Deliver the Appropriate Leadership Style**

   Then

5. **Begin to manage the journey to group empowerment**

*Adapted from R.B. Lacoursiere, *The Life Cycle of Groups: Group Developmental Stage Theory* (New York: Human Service Press, 1980).

Maria found that becoming an effective team leader was exciting, challenging, but not simple. It took time, persistence and commitment on her part. Being a good team leader was much harder than being an autocratic leader. She learned that when you want to empower people it is exhausting to get them ready to share responsibility. "It takes less energy to say 'my way or the highway,'" she reflected. "It's not for the fainthearted, but the results are worth it."

Dan and Maria kept in contact ever since their sessions with the One Minute Manager. They enjoyed comparing their learnings with each other.

"I think sharing all the concepts with my work unit has been the biggest help," said Maria one day. "I told them everything I learned from you and the One Minute Manager about groups. I wanted everyone to know the stages of group development so that the burden for helping the group move from one stage to the next did not all lie with me."

Sharing It With Others / 109

"Did they help with your diagnosis, too?" asked Dan.

"They sure did," answered Maria, "and it was fun too. They made comments like: 'Here we are in Stage 2!' Then once we all knew what stage the group was in, everyone helped provide the direction and support that was needed."

"I bet your folks really keep you honest, don't they?" asked Dan.

Maria smiled, "They make sure I adopt the appropriate style of leadership. But the one thing that is even more important than having my work unit involved in diagnosis and adaptability is the feeling of empowerment we all have gotten. No one is concerned if I am late or miss a meeting. They can assume leadership and I feel a new freedom and trust."

"That would really make the One Minute Manager feel happy," said Dan. "He's always told us that:

*

EMPOWERMENT

IS

ALL ABOUT

<u>LETTING GO</u>

SO THAT

OTHERS CAN

<u>GET GOING</u>

*

The End

Praisings

We would like to give credit to the following people whose conceptual contributions were invaluable to us in preparing this book.

Ken Benne and *Paul Sheats* for their pioneering work on functional roles of group members.

Paul Hersey for his creative work with Ken Blanchard in the development of Situational Leadership theory.

Irving Janis for his development and documentation of the Groupthink concept.

R. B. Lacoursiere for his thorough analysis of the life cycle of groups.

Marshall Sashkin for his courageous argument about participation as an ethical imperative.

Edgar Schein for his clear thinking about process consultation and group observation.

Jessie Stoner for her contributions to the PERFORM model.

National Training Labs Institute for its pioneering work in group dynamics and group development and for the significant impact that organization has had on all of our lives.

We are also thankful for the thoughtful reviews and critiques of:

Blanchard Training and Development Associates, including *Marjorie Blanchard, Calla Crafts, Fred Finch, Laurie Hawkins, Alan Randolph, Ruth Anne Randolph, Rick Tate, Pat Zigarmi and Drea Zigarmi*.

University of Massachusetts doctoral students too numerous to mention individually for their challenging and constructive feedback and suggestions.

The many participants in High-Performing Team seminars and management development programs who reviewed earlier drafts of the manuscript and suggested several important changes.

In addition we would like to express our sincere thanks to *Eleanor Terndrup, Lisa Hendricsen, Katy Clawson, Harry Paul,* and especially *Gene Kira* and *Anya D'Alessio* for making a timely production of this book possible.

And finally to *Robert Nelson* whose patience, guidance and appropriate nudging made it all happen.

About the Authors

Few individuals have impacted the day-to-day management of people and companies as has **Ken Blanchard**.

A gregarious, sought-after and prominent author, speaker and business consultant, he is universally characterized by friends, colleagues and clients as one of the most insightful, powerful and compassionate men in business today. A multitude of Fortune 500 companies and fast-growing entrepreneurial enterprises have benefited from his unique approach to managing and developing people.

As a writer in the field of management, his impact has been far-reaching. His One Minute Manager Library, which includes *The One Minute Manager* (1982), *Putting the One Minute Manager to Work* (1984), *Leadership and the One Minute Manager* (1985), *The One Minute Manager Gets Fit* (1986), and *The One Minute Manager Meets the Monkey* (1989) has collectively sold more than 7 million copies and has been translated into more than 20 languages. He is also co-author with Dr. Paul Hersey of *Management of Organizational Behavior*, a classic textbook now in its fifth edition, and of *The Power of Ethical Management* (1988) with Dr. Norman Vincent Peale.

Blanchard is chairman of Blanchard Training and Development, Inc., a full-service management consulting and training company which he founded in 1979 with his wife Marjorie. He also maintains a faculty position in leadership at the University of

Massachusetts, Amherst and a visiting lectureship at Cornell University, where he is also an elected member of the Board of Trustees.

He has been a guest on a number of national television programs, including "Good Morning America" and "The Today Show," and has been featured in *Time, People, U.S. News & World Report* and a host of other popular publications. He is also a contributing editor of *Executive Excellence* newsletter.

He earned his B.A. in government and philosophy from Cornell University, his M.A. in sociology and counseling from Colgate University and his Ph.D. in educational administration and leadership from Cornell University.

Don Carew is an accomplished and respected management consultant, trainer and educator and a dynamic motivational speaker.

He has consulted with governmental, educational and business organizations throughout the United States, Mexico, and Canada and specializes in the areas of leadership, team building, organization change, employee involvement and collaboration in work settings.

His keynote addresses and seminars are presented with enthusiasm and humor and are built upon knowledge and hands-on experience. He is often regarded as genuine and caring and relates well to any audience regardless of the diversity of its members.

He is a full-time professor in the Division of Human Services and Applied Behavioral Sciences at the University of Massachusetts and also directs the Group Organizational Studies doctoral program.

He is co-creator of the High Performing Teams product line offered by Blanchard Training and Development and has authored a multitude of articles for professional journals. He is also an active associate of the NTL Institute.

He holds a bachelor's degree in business from Ohio University, a master's degree in human relations from Ohio University and a doctorate in counseling psychology from the University of Florida.

Eunice Parisi-Carew is an accomplished management consultant and trainer and a sought-after motivational speaker.

With a broad base of experience in many facets of management and organizational development, she has designed, directed and implemented training and consulting projects for a number of top North American corporations, including Merrill Lynch, AT&T, Hyatt Hotels, Transco Energy Company and the Department of Health, Education and Welfare.

As a speaker, she connects instantly with an audience. She exudes sincerity and knowledge and keeps people involved and interested. She is perceptive to a group's needs and is often described as articulate, engaging and humorous.

Team building, leadership, productivity improvement, ethics, customer service and life management are among the many topics she addresses in seminars, speeches and articles. She is also co-creator of the High Performing Teams product line offered by Blanchard Training and Development.

She has directed a graduate program in Group Dynamics and Leadership at the University of Hartford and is a part-time faculty member of American University. She is also a member of the Board of Directors of the NTL Institute. She is currently the vice president of Professional Services at Blanchard Training and Development.

She received her Ed.D. in behavioral sciences from the University of Massachusetts, and is also a licensed psychologist in the state of Massachusetts.

Services Available

Blanchard Training and Development, Inc. (BTD) is a full-service training and consulting company in the areas of team development, leadership, customer service, performance management, ethics and wellness.

BTD offers training services as well as a complete product line on the topic of Building High Performing Teams™ that combines the fundamentals of group dynamics with core skills of team building. This program has served as a primary benefit to organizations of every type and size in helping to increase organizational productivity through its focus upon the development of effective work teams.

Building High Performing Teams™ includes the foundation concepts of Situational Leadership® II, one of the leading management development models of our time, that will help guide your teams to maximum performance.

To find out more information about Building High Performing Teams™ or other BTD products, seminars or counsulting services, please call or write:

Blanchard Training and Development, Inc.
125 State Place, Escondido, CA 92025
(800) 728-6000 or (619) 489-5005